Derbyshire Children at Home 1800-1900

DERBYSHIRE CHILDREN AT HOME

E.G. POWER

Scarthin Books
Cromford
2003

Published 2003
by Scarthin Books of Cromford, Derbyshire
©2003 E.G. Power

website: http://www.scarthinbooks.demon.co.uk
email: clare@scarthinbooks.demon.co.uk

Typesetting and design by
Elisabeth Stoppard and Mike Susko
Set in Monotype Scala by
Masson Multimedia, Bonsall, Derbyshire

No part of this book may be reproduced in any
form by any means without the permission of
the owner of the copyright.

ISBN 1 9000446 05 7

Printed by Bell & Bain Ltd, Glasgow

Contents

Cover, George Ashton Strutt, aged about 9 ; with his father George Herbert and grandfather, George Henry

Frontispiece, George Ashton Strutt, aged about 9

Acknowledgements

To Belper Historical Society for permission to use the Strutt Family group.

To the County and Diocesan Archivist for obtaining permission to quote from family records.

To the staff of Derbyshire Record Office and Derbyshire Diocesan Record Office for their enthusiastic help to the author in his researches.

To Sir Richard FitzHerbert (Bart.) of Tissington Hall for permission to photograph family portraits.

To James Cartland of Carnfield Hall for permission to photograph his collection of children's toys.

Copies of records in Derbyshire County Council's County Record Office are reproduced by permission of the County and Diocesan Archivist.

Reference numbers of quoted material will be given in a copy of this book which will be available in the Record Office soon after publication.

Dramatis Personæ – The main characters

The FitzHerberts of Tissington Hall

Sir Henry FitzHerbert was one of four children of Sir William FitzHerbert and Sarah Perrin. The other three were Anthony, George and Fanny. Anthony and George predeceased Henry, who inherited Tissington Hall and Farleigh in Kent. Lady Agnes was one of the Beresford family; her father was Vicar of Ashbourne. Her mother lived at Tissington Hall after the marriage of Henry and Agnes. Their marriage took place in 1805. Their children, with years of birth, are as follows:

Selina	1806
William	1808
Richard	1809
Alleyne	1815
Maria	1816
Anthony	1818
John	1820
Judith	1821
Fanny	1823
Augusta	1828

The FitzHerberts were Derbyshire landowners. They also had sugar estates in the West Indies and, for some years, a house in Henrietta Street, London; but they were not enormously rich, with ten children – five boys to be educated at Charterhouse or Harrow, and the University, and five girls to be provided with dowries. Lady Agnes managed her household expenses judiciously. When Sir Henry was planning his first visit to the West Indies, his uncle, Alleyne FitzHerbert, Lord St Helens, warned him that the cost, one way, would be about £120, but he offered a little financial help, in the most delicate terms:

> I happen to be possessed of £300 for which I have no earthly use, and shall think myself much obliged by your taking this little sum off my hands either by way of loan or gift as you may be pleased to determine.

Sir Henry was a JP and Sheriff for Derbyshire in 1815 and took a full share in County affairs: Derby and Chesterfield races, Ashbourne Savings Bank, inspecting gaols, supporting concerts, charities, and turnpike roads. He took a close interest in his children's upbringing, and in his tenants' and his own farming. His Diaries contain many entries such as: "Began my hay, very good crops"; "The red cow calved"; "On the 11th the sow pigged 10 young ones"; "Went to Mr Dales at Lea Hall to see a very large Pig". And, an important event: April 20th 1829, "William Johnson, & escort, in a cart took the Alderney Bull to Calke Abbey & brought back another Bull from Sir George Crewe's".

As a subscriber (and President in 1835) to Derby Infirmary, Sir Henry had the right to nominate anyone for treatment there – reassuring for the villagers. Among the papers is a note from his son, Alleyne, in April 1844, asking him to write a request for Michael Turner, an Irish cattle drover, "who has been injured inwardly...to be admitted In-patient at the Infirmary".

Lady Agnes provided her own medical services in the village, as she saw fit:

15 Jan 1834

> We have still rain rain rain & many applications in the village for Brandy for the stomach ache. I have sent peppermint & rhubarb mixture instead.

5 Feb 1840

> My patients are all better except George Redfern's baby who has got a gathering in the Ear...

She also tried to provide some education for the village children:

20 Sept 1827

> I have quite settled my School and it will open next Monday.

The FitzHerbert material includes some 1,200 letters covering an early period, 1740 to 1794, and a later period, 1819 to 1880. Most of Sir Henry's Diaries survive for the period 1808 to 1858. There are also some miscellaneous documents, not particularly relating to children.

The D'Ewes Coke Family

Their home was Brookhill Hall, near Alfreton. Their father, D'Ewes Coke, was a landowner and barrister, whose father had been Rector of Pinxton and South Normanton. Their mother, Harriet Wright of Mapperley, died in 1815. The children, with years of birth, are as follows:

Tissington Hall

(Harriet) Frances	1800
Elizabeth	1802
(Francis Lillyman) D'Ewes	1804
William	1805
Edward	1807
(Sarah) Sophia: "Sophy"	1808
(Mary) Agnes	1809
Emma	1810
(John) Henry	1811
Richard	1813

The main sources are three Diaries: of D'Ewes Coke the Elder for 1817; the Diary or "Log Book" of the Governess for 1818; and another Diary of the father which runs only from January to 3rd September 1820. There are also a few letters from 1813 to 1819.

Longsdon and Lace

The Longsdon family of Little Longstone were quite substantial farmers. James Longsdon married Elizabeth Gardom in 1785. They had three sons, James, John and William, and a daughter, Kate.

James had a daughter by Maria Lees in 1811, but refused to marry her. He did marry Anne Oates in 1825, had a son Henry John in 1826, and died in 1827. In December 1851, this son, now Rev. Henry John Longsdon, married Frances Dorothea Lace, of Ingthorpe Grange,

Skipton. She was the elder sister of J W Lace. Strictly speaking, J W Lace does not qualify as a "Derbyshire child", but has been made one by grace and favour of the author.

The D'EwesCoke family at Brookhill Hall

The letters fall into three main groups: 1799-1810, when the three Longsdon boys were away at school; 1814-1815 between Maria and James; and 1841-1849 between J W and Fanny (Frances). In all there are about 40 letters.

The Arkwright Boys

Richard, Robert, Peter and Charles were the sons of Richard Arkwright II and grandsons of Sir Richard Arkwright, the cotton magnate of Cromford. There are some 12 letters mostly relating to the boating fracas at Eton 1797-1802. There are also a few letters of Frederic, son of Peter Arkwright, 1816-1821.

The Wager Family

William Wager, who died in 1869, was a well-off farmer of Great Longstone. He owned more than 70 acres of land, and left £300 each to his three youngest children when they should reach the age of twenty-five. Harriet, born in 1848, went to boarding school in Bakewell and at Bubnell Hall. The letters are mostly from the 1860s, but many were obviously written as school exercises. The material also includes a number of printed books for children of that period.

William and Richard Turbutt

Their father, Gladwin Turbutt, was a wealthy landowner, living at Ogston Hall. He was High Sheriff of Derbyshire in 1858. He and his wife, Ellen, had two sons, William and Richard. The collection contains about 120 letters mostly from the boys at Harrow and prior to that at a school in Brighton, including a bill for repairing wallpaper "behind the door in Schoolroom, consequent upon having been daubed with ink".

George Strutt and his sisters

George Ashton Strutt's father was George Herbert Strutt, of Bridgehill House, Brailsford House, Makeney House and Kingairloch Estate, Argyll. Herbert Strutt, as he was usually known, was the grandson of Jedediah Strutt, founder of the highly profitable cotton-spinning firm in Belper and Milford. George Herbert married Edith Adela Yelverton in 1876. George Ashton was born in 1878; his elder sister Adela was born in 1877 and Isabel in 1881. The letters, about 130, run from 1889

Willersley Castle

to 1895. Most of them are from George, at school in Brighton and at Harrow. There are a few written by Adela and Isabel.

The Rich and The Poor

The terms "rich" and "poor" are, of course, imprecise. The author defends his use of them by reference to Benjamin Disraeli. In 1845 he published his novel "Sybil" with the subtitle "The Two Nations", which were, as one of the characters declared, The Rich and The Poor.

Ogston Hall

Until the coming of cheap elementary education one might easily substitute the labels "literate" and "illiterate" for "rich" and "poor". It is a truism that the rich wrote about themselves and to each other, in diaries, memoirs and letters, and that the poor were written about, in occasional brief references, or as the subject of some official enquiry into working or living conditions. A poor child who could later write his own life story, like William Hutton of Derby, was a rarity. The relatively short space given in this book to poor children at home is due to this lack of evidence.

6

New Arrivals

Fortunate babies

> ...both Selina and the baby quite well, but we could not get enough from dear Selina to support the dear Baby...and therefore we have got a very nice young Woman in the Village to suckle our little one, and hers, which is two months old, suckes Selina ...
>
> Lady Agnes FitzHerbert on her first grandchild, June 1831.

Babies born to the FitzHerberts in the early 19th century were very fortunate in being welcomed into a family whose members all took pride and delight in the newcomer.

On 23rd November 1823 Lady Agnes FitzHerbert's ninth child was born. Three weeks later she wrote to Sir Henry who was away at the time:

> Dearest Henry,
>
> ...Baby looking beautiful   she has had a little Rhubarb powder & something warming to the stomach in it, and she laughed all day &

Bathtime

slept all night but Dr. Sims has sent me two wet Nurses & I am waiting at this moment to see them, as he says he fears it will be found to be the milk that disagrees... [The baby's stomach had been upset]. ...I have just seen them and did not like either – the powder he gave the Baby has quite corrected the little acidity...

He thinks the Nurse we have a very good one and with (as he says) a good country constitution...I am very careful & very anxious to be well and have all the dear Bairns well to present to you on your return...

Adieu my dear dear own Henry

Ever yr faithful & affte wife AF

On 18th December she wrote again:

...the Baby is delightful, her Bowels quite well...last night...as I had closed the shutters & was amusing myself with the Baby in the Drawing room Lord St. Helens arrived in the midst of the Wind & Rain, on foot, on purpose to see me   he was so gay and so agreeable, admired the Baby & sat with me an hour...

Two days later Lady Agnes wrote another short progress report: "...the Baby is perfection & takes no powders and does all properly". On 22nd December she wrote with further news:

...I was at Church this morning, took dear Baby who behaved nicely. She is now Frances Rafella...

A year later Sir Henry was absent again, this time on his way to the West Indies. In a letter dated Xmas day 1824 Lady Agnes wrote about the baby's progress:

...dear little Fanny I wish you could see   she twines in and out between the tables and chairs, & takes great care of herself – she calls papa, & says many little words – no no &c   last night when she heard the Xmas Hymn she said Oh dear...

In January 1828 Lady Agnes wrote to Sir Henry telling him about a slight upset for Fanny (now 3) about which she had consulted Dr Greaves. She continued, mysteriously, "I did not ask him about myself...I think I know, as well as he can tell me, what is the matter!!"

In her next letter she was still treating the matter with some delicacy:

I mentioned my feelings to Dr Greaves, and he says there is not the least doubt on the subject...I have had woeful nights but I shall, I dare say, sleep better when I have my own old dear companion who loves me by my side.

In August Maria (nearly 12) was writing from Farleigh to "My dear Papa...Give my love to Mama...and a kiss to dear little Fanny and tell her we are all well and long to know whether Baby is arrived".

Baby did arrive early in September. Sir Henry's Diary records:

Sept 2 1828 Agnes went to her bedroom at ¹/₂ past 12.

Dr Davis came at ¹/₄ before 7 in the morning. Another daughter born at ¹/₂ past 3pm.

John (8) and Judith (10) both wrote to Sir Henry from Farleigh on 4th September. Judith wrote, "My dear Papa, I must wish you and every body joy, and hope Mama and little Sister are quite well. Pray tell me what color her eyes are, and what her name is going to be".

John (8) had his own perspective on the subject of his new baby sister. He wrote, "I am very happy dear Mama has given us a little sister we all long to see..." and went on briskly to write about his new puppy.

In October Selina (22), who was staying at Somersal Hall, wrote to Lady Agnes in her usual style. Referring to Sir Henry's sister, Fanny, she continued:

I wish she would come down with you – I think she ought to help to chaperone this new bairn they all talk so about here – has my Aunt pinched up its nose? – we have great expectations on the score of its beauty, so mind you feed it up well & keep its legs straight, & its little face polished & its bows in trim order & its capborders plaited to a T.

In December, by which time the parents had still not decided on a name, Selina wrote again. "A kiss to dear little Finfan & she may give one for me to little <u>Nameless</u>. I am quite sorry that it cannot be Isabella..."

On 21st January 1829 the new baby, now four months old, was still nameless. Lady Agnes wrote to Sir Henry in London:

...all the dear Chicks are well...I think it prudent this severe weather to keep them in the house, all except Johnny [8] who has at present escaped. Will you be so good as to buy for us a handsome Ivory Cup & Ball. You will get the best at that good toy shop in Bond Street. <u>Be sure to bring one</u>.

Before long, however, the question of the name was settled. We find Anthony, back at school, writing: "Love to all and a kiss to little Augusta, and I hope a smile from her".

In a letter of 24th September 1829 we get a picture of Augusta at just a year old, in a letter of Lady Agnes to Sir Henry:

> The Wrights & Beresfords are to dine with us on Saturday & I am such a goose that I cannot bear to wean dear little Gussy before that day lest she should lose a particle of her plump cheeks, or charm, or sweet smile   she has been the merriest little thing this evening, and she calls out, when we ask her where Papa is, Oh dear! Do you love him? we say and she answers by <u>kissing the air</u>.

The following day Lady Agnes wrote again:

> ...little Gussy too looks for you everywhere   she is at this moment on Miss Pohlman's [the governess] knee in her little night Chemise looking like a rose – she has got a double tooth and on Tuesday next we are resolved to wean her.

A few days later Lady Agnes wrote again on the subject of Gussy:

> I must tell you the prettiest little story about her   whilst I was dressing she crept away and I could not see her anywhere but I heard her in the Drawing Room calling out <u>Papa</u>, <u>Papa</u>, & she crawled to your picture & was rearing herself up upon her little hands with her head up, looking just at the picture & calling out <u>Papa</u>.

In less than two years Augusta had been deprived of her status as the new baby. Her elder sister Selina married Frank Wright in August 1830, and in June 1831 Lady Agnes was staying with them at Lamcote. She wrote to announce the birth of a grandson, and told Sir Henry, "It is impossible for any two people to be going on better than our dear Child and Grandchild". On 23rd June she wrote again:

> ...dear Selina has passed the third day with a pulse as calm as if nothing had happened and not even a headache or a restless night...I never saw a nicer baby, not even one of our own...you never heard anything like the Compliments paid me   a poor woman in the village...upon hearing I was the Granny said Lord bless me,

what a <u>well favoured Woman you are</u>. Frank, [she added] thinks there never was such a <u>lad</u> as his...

A couple of days later, Sir Henry, staying with his uncle, Lord St Helen's, in London, was given one of his frequent shopping chores:

Selina would be pleased if you brought her little lad a little wee hat...it must be white <u>Bersimere</u> a very neat one and a very small sized one...remember it must be a Boy's <u>Hat</u> & not a Girl's Bonnet. His name is to be John which I dare say you have supposed... [Frank Wright's father was John].

The proud grandmother's next letter to Sir Henry on 26th June was full of more news about the baby: how the feeding problem was solved; the doctor's advice; the inadequacy of the nurse; and the reception of the news in Tissington:

...both Selina & the baby quite well, but we could not get enough from dear Selina to support the dear baby, supposing it able to get it, & therefore we have got a very nice young Woman in the Village to suckle our little one, and hers which is two months old suckes Selina and drains her breasts to perfection...

...[she] is very good about keeping in Bed which Mr. William Wright the Doctor advises & says is much more essential after these easy, quick labours than after a severe one...he seems a most skilful man...quite a treasure...as to the Nurse she is the greatest ignoramus & the most stupid Woman I ever saw...she knows no more about them than – I am quite at a loss for a simile.

...I have such accounts from Tissington of the joy which spread, they say, like wildfire through the Village the bells rang for an hour.

The next day Lady Agnes wrote to Mrs James Hardy, for many years Nanny at Tissington Hall, referring to Selina as "your dear Nursling" and giving more details of the birth:

She was really taken with her first pain at $^1/_2$ past four o'clock in the morning and her Baby was born at _ before seven. I never was more astonished than when I heard it cry...I had no idea there could have been such a calm, quiet entrance into the world – it seems almost like a dream.

Lady Agnes was again scathing about the nurse:

> Such an ignorant creature never, I believe, before undertook the nursing but we are going to pack her off tomorrow – I have been a Dragon over her & made her do all I bid about the dear baby, but such a creature, you would have laughed had you seen her attempt to give the baby a drop of Castor oil & she confessed she never gave a young child Physick before we shall amuse you with Nursing histories when we meet.

Maria (14) wrote to Sir Henry on 26th June wishing him "joy upon the birth of your dear little Grandson and our Nephew". Judith (9) added a few words "to wish you joy on the birth of our little Gentleman who we all long to nurse". John (11) wrote. "For fear you should think I had forgotten you, my dear Papa, I put a few words to the others to wish you joy, joy, joy, of the little boy, boy, boy. Grannie has been so happy ever since she became great Granny that she is quite cracky, as she says". Alleyne, preparing to go to university, enquired, "What is the name of our nebby to be?" And William wrote from Athlone Barracks in Ireland to ask, "If Maria is with you pray tell her I should like to set up a correspondance with her...I expect her nephew will afford matter for two sheets at least".

In November 1831 Selina wrote to her little sister Gussy (3) about her little nephew John, now five months old:

> I must write to tell you that I hope your little nephew will soon come to see you – as I hear you say he ought to do – He is grown quite a man, & does not lie down now in nurse's arms, but sits upright & is in short petticoats. He looks about at everything & will like his grand Papa's bright gold watch & twinkling seals very much - & he laughs & is so merry, I am sure that you will love him.

A year later Selina was reporting to her father on his grandson's progress. Referring to a visit from her husband's family, she wrote:

> Dear little Johnnie behaved himself à merveille amongst all his Aunts, & dear Mrs. Wright is almost as fond and foolish a grandmamma as mylady [Lady Agnes]. Johnnie is beginning to venture alone – his very great care of himself & precaution is called by his flatterers prudence – but it looks a little cowardly to my impartial eye...

Before moving on to some less fortunate babies, another letter from Selina to her father is worth quoting. It refers to the birth of her seventh child in 1840, and mentions one of the minor problems of large families – finding names for so many children. It is also worth quoting because Selina's letters are as entertaining now as her family thought then. The baby girl, she says,

> is particularly healthy & plumpy & strengthy...seems to me to promise well as a worthy daughter of her papa, the Signor Allegro...Now for our youngster's name – we must not discard Mary, because besides all the bygone, worthy Marys in the Wright Family, & the good old one still extant, our baby is named after our great grandmother Mary Meynell...then we thought of tacking Jane to it...Joan does not come to me with a good grace...so what is to be done? We must have the Bishop [nickname of her brother Alleyne] for the Godfather...I keep still a good deal to the doctor's favourite horizontal position – only out of prudence for I am very well.

Not all pregnancies were trouble-free, even in the FitzHerbert family. Lady Agnes herself lost her fourth baby, in December 1810. Sir Henry's Diary records: "On the 18th Lady Fitzherbert was brought to bed of a boy who died very soon after he was born".

In 1788 Henry Gally, a relative of Sir William FitzHerbert (Sir Henry's father), wrote to tell him that Mrs Gally had borne him a son. "She had not a short labour, for it lasted nineteen hours". (Three years previously she had given birth to a stillborn boy after two days). "She certainly does not go thro' these Businesses vigorously" was her husband's unsympathetic comment.

Babies born into poor families had, on the whole, a lower chance of survival, particularly in large towns. Doctors were out of the question, nurses and midwives were self-appointed and gravely unreliable, and knowledge of hygiene was very rudimentary.

Born out of wedlock

Babies born to unmarried women faced even greater hazards. This was especially so if the father "disappeared" or refused to acknowledge the child as his. If this happened the baby might simply be abandoned by its mother, hopefully to be found by someone before it died. It could then be looked after by the Parish authorities, or it might be cared for by grandparents or other relatives, or (more commonly in works of

fiction) by some wealthy philanthropist. In extreme cases a desperate
mother might try to solve her problem by killing the baby, as Mary
Dilkes did. Her crime and her punishment were reported in the Derby
Mercury in 1754:

> *Derby, March 28*
>
> Last Saturday, betwixt Twelve and One o'clock, Mary Dilkes was,
> (pursuant to her sentence at the late Assizes for the Murder of a
> Bastard Child) carried in a cart from the Gaoler's House to the
> usual place of Execution, where, after spending some time in
> Devotion, being assisted therein by a Clergyman, she was executed,
> amidst a vast number of Spectators.

Most mothers, of course, wanted to keep their babies, and if the father
was willing to pay for its keep, it was fairly lucky. On 11th April 1757,
John Smith (his actual name!) of Alfreton scaled a Bond for "one
hundred pounds of lawful Money of Great Britain" to be paid to the
Churchwardens and Overseers of the Poor of the Parish, if he failed to
provide for "the future Maintenance, Education, Nourishment and
bringing up of the said Female Bastard Child..." The Parish officials in
this case noted to their "good liking and satisfaction" (and also no
doubt to that of the mother, Ann Leavers) that John Smith had already
"took care and provided for the said Child and paid all such Costs,
Charges and Expenses...concerning the Birth and Maintenance" of the
baby up to the date of the Bond.

A Bastardy Bond like this was the usual method by which the Parish
Overseers ensured that illegitimate children did not have to be provided
for out of the Parish Rates. If the father was not very well off, or
unreliable, another person might be included as a guarantor. So, on
14th January 1783, as "Mary Tafft...Singlewoman, hath declared that
she is with Child or Children...and that Edward Hollingworth the
Younger is the father". Edward Hollingworth the Elder and Edward
Hollingworth the Younger, both of Melbourne, bound themselves in
£80 that they would "indemnify and save harmless" the Parish of
Stanton-by-Bridge where Mary lived "from all manner of costs and
charges".

Another method was for the Parish authorities to get a Bastardy Order,
signed by two Justices of the Peace, ordering the unmarried father to
pay a weekly fixed sum to the Overseers (not directly to the mother). An
Order of 1797 "concerning a Male Bastard Child lately born on the

Body of Dolley Smedley of Youlgreave" required Benjamin Rickards, the father, to pay "the Sum of £1-19-0 for and towards the lying-in...and the maintenance...to the [present] time" and in future "three shillings & sixpence weekly and every week from this present time". If Dolley Smedley was unable or unwilling to look after the child herself, Benjamin was to pay an extra "one Shilling and Ninepence" weekly. In a similar case in "Yolgrave" in 1810, it was the mother, Ann Oldfield, who would have to pay the Overseers an extra shilling a week if she did not "nurse and take care of" the child herself. In such cases the baby would be cared for by some poor woman of the Parish, paid a small fee by the Overseers.

Having babies out of wedlock was not, of course, confined to the lower classes. Sir Henry Harpur of Calke Abbey (1763-1819) made provision for his "natural" children by "Sarah Chamberlayne, Spinster, now residing at Repton". A series of bonds survives, which illustrate his concern. One dated 1777 provided that, in the event of his death, Sarah was to have £100 per year, and was also to keep the house in which she was living, with all its furniture and other contents. In 1780 he arranged for his daughter Lucy Chamberlayne to have £15 a year until she was six, £20 from then until she was twelve, and from then until she was twenty-one she was to have the interest of £1,000 at 4%.

The same terms were made for Elizabeth and Henry. John was to get £25 per year up to the age of fourteen and then 4% interest on £1,000 until he was twenty-one. In 1788 Sir Henry provided that a daughter, Frances, and a yet unborn child, both by Frances Farrand of Barnes, Surrey, should each have £500 with interest at 5%.

These children were well provided for by this very wealthy and eccentric but obviously considerate man. Where the father was well off, but irresponsible, an illegitimate child was in a much less desirable situation.

James Longsdon, of Longstone, was a well-to-do farmer, wealthy enough to send his eldest son, James, to boarding school, first at Heath and then in Nottingham. A series of letters survives, dating from May 1814, sent to James by Maria Lees. James, then aged 28, was living at home with his parents. Maria (significantly signing herself Maria Longsdon) was living with her father in Lancashire. Maria's mother was dead, but the third member of the family was a little girl called Harriet. Harriet's existence is explained by a remark in Maria's letter of

6th July 1814: "It is four years this very day since Ellen Barnsley's Wedding. I little thought then of the trials I must have undergone or I should not have been so saucy..."

Maria tried every means to persuade James to marry her. Unwisely, on one of his rare visits, she allowed, or encouraged, him to father another child on her, but to no avail. Her father was angry with her, and she was rarely allowed to see Harriet, who lived with the Hudsons, mother and daughter, "which my Father keeps".

James seemed to want to postpone marriage until he inherited the family farm, and various relatives advised Maria to be patient, but in May 1814 she wrote:

Swearing in before a J.P

> I lead a life more miserable than a dog, I am a complete prisoner never going out nor seeing anyone that comes and before I will live in this state of suspence I will...marry a working man that would bring me his wages home weekly, and lay on a bed of Straw for peace and contentment".

On 6th July 1914 she sent him "a bit of my darling's hair", and ended her letter "My dear Love though unhappy, your M..Longsdon".

Her letter of 28th July contained an account of the birth of their son. She had "such violent pains" that they sent for the doctor "who ordered...a bladder of warm water applied to my side..." "my little Lad was put to Nurse the night after he was born and my Father said he insisted upon them never bringing him...into his sight anywhere...my dear Innocents I fear are in the <u>Wasps nest</u>". She added bitterly, "from your last letter it plainly appears to me that there is no more prospect of our being married" and suggested that he should please his parents by finding a wealthy wife "as Riches seem the only quality to please them".

She concluded by asking "...that a Provision may be settled upon, for the children..." and added "I mean to have the little one baptized in a few days who I purpose calling <u>James</u> after his Father who he will perhaps never see..." This thought was soon to become fact in a way that Maria had not imagined.

About a fortnight later she wrote again:

> Dear James,
>
> You will be surprized to receive another letter from me...last Thursday week my little Boy was taken ill... the Dr. visited him daily and administered every thing to give him relief...it pleased the Almighty to take him out of his pain last Saturday morning, he was very patient although he had convulsion Fits inwardly, he was too good for this wicked world.

It was some comfort that Maria's father was sympathetic, and arranged that little James should have a proper funeral.

> He was Buried in a neat, genteel manner on Tuesday at St. John's Church, and with as much Attention as if he had been grown a man...

All this time Harriet (now nearly four) was still living with the Hudsons, the "Nurse" and her daughter who was "kept" by Maria's father. Harriet saw her mother every Sunday, when the Hudsons visited, and James sent some money, now and then, but Maria still had hopes of marriage or at least a legal settlement and regular payments for Harriet.

In November she wrote to James again, mentioning that her father was going to visit him, and thanking him for a hare he had sent them: "...it was the best I ever eat as tender as a chicken". In another chatty and optimistic letter in December Maria assured him that she would "never have the same affection for any other man" and concluded:

> You would be quite entertained to hear my little chatterbox, her tongue seldom lies still, I am in hopes of seeing her to-day at dinner.
>
> your ever affectionate
>
> M. Longsdon

James was still not to be moved, however, and sadly but understandably, Maria became more bitter, although she was normally light-hearted. (Mentioning a cousin of hers whom she had met, she wrote: "he is such a scantifyed [sic] Methodist I cannot make that mirth with him I otherwise should").

Early in March 1815 she wrote complaining:

> ...the last Money you remitted me...there was four pounds odd owing to the woman, which is the case now, besides a Doctor's Bill of £- I know not, for [Harriet] has been very dangerously ill of a worm Fever which held her near two months her life was at one time despaired of...and indeed once I took my leave never expecting to see her more on this side the Grave a great many died of the same complaint, however it pleased God to restore her.

The next letter, on 27th March, ominously began, not with "dear James" but "Mr Jas. Longsdon, Sir", and stated, "I am determined upon having a settlement made for <u>your Child</u> before I leave the neighbourhood". Just over a week later she wrote from Broughton, not to James but to his mother. The Poor Law system had begun to catch up with Maria and Harriet, or at least, so she told Mrs Longsdon. The "old Nurse", she said, "informed me that the Overseer of Broughton had been...and said that unless my father would give security to the Parish they should have me removed and immediately too, to the Parish the Father of her belonged" (i.e., Longstone).

Harriet was now nearly five. She thought of the Nurse, Mrs Hudson, as her grandmother, but as Maria wrote, "she now comes to have so much sense that she is ruining..." It appears that the threatened scandal of Maria and Harriet being removed to Longstone, to be kept by the Parish, proved more than James could stomach. The letters come to an end, presumably because he finally made a settlement on which Maria and Harriet could live.

Harriet's misfortunes, however, did not end there. One last document in the collection is entitled Mr Finch's Agreement. Mr Finch was a solicitor mentioned earlier in one of Maria's letters. But this is not the settlement made in 1815. It is dated 4th April 1823, when Harriet was thirteen, and it refers to "Harriet Longsdon the natural Child of the late Maria Lees". It is an agreement made by James Longsdon with "Esther Goodair of Salford in the parish of Manchester" by which Esther undertakes to keep Harriet for three years "...with Meat, drink, Cloathes, washing and Lodging, also to Instruct or get instructed the said Child in Reading, Writing, Sewing and common Arithetic [sic] in consideration of which...James Longsdon agrees to pay...the sum of five Shillings per Week...in Quarterly payments..." Not at all a generous allowance when we remember that in 1797 Benjamin Rickards of Youlgrave would have had to pay a total of five shillings and threepence a week to have his child taken care of.

A workman's cottage

Little Children

Master Richard has amused himself both last evening and this, by sitting on the side of the Pond and putting his feet in the water, stockings & shoes inclusive.

Richard: I long to see Henry come home, but then he'll beat me, so I do not think I want him.

D'Ewes Coke children, from the Governess' Diary, 1818.

The things they do and say

At the beginning of the year 1818, when Miss Burgess, Governess in the D'Ewes Coke household at Brookhill Hall, began her record of the children's work and behaviour, Richard was almost five, Henry was just turned seven, Emma was seven and Agnes eight and a half. There were two older children at home.

Richard had a reputation for saying "clever" things:

Saturday, 24th January
> Richard got a <u>Bump</u> a day or two ago, on his forehead, by running against a wall. The Swelling extended to his upper eyelid, he was told it had made his eye less. He replied: he did not care – he could see as well out of a little eye as a big one.

April was the time to begin tending their own little garden plots, but there were not enough tools to go round. Miss Burgess recorded:

> Richard is still, when good, our most amusing companion. He told his brother and sisters that he had planted a nail in his garden and he thought perhaps it might grow to a spade. [She added, rather unnecessarily] This was a witticism upon their want of garden tools, and his droll manner did not let us suppose it proceeded from ignorance.

In October 1818, when Henry was away from home for a fortnight, Miss Burgess recorded Richard's reactions:

Little Children

Friday 16th

Master Richard playing "the spoiled child" he seems to think that because he is "alone" as he expresses himself, he is to be made quite a Pet.

Sunday 18th

...he asked me if, when I was a little girl & my little sister went out, I did not feel "alone"...at present he seems not to have forgotten him for a moment.

Wednesday 21st

Master Richard continues to make regular enquiries respecting Henry's return...

Tuesday 27th

Master Richard does not know whether he should rejoice, or not, at his brother's return. He said yesterday, "I long to see Henry come home, but then he'll beat me, so I do not think I want him".

Wednesday 28th

Neither of the little boys have been good today...Henry has not quite exhausted his stock of news.

Henry could at times be quite as precocious as Richard. One Sunday in September 1818 Miss Burgess reported:

H. & R. were not quite correct in their conduct at Church. [A few days earlier] Master H. met Mr. Wilson during the week and begged him "not to read so much at Church". He thought "Seven pages were quite enough & he was sure Mr.W. read a hundred".

A frequent punishment for one of the children was to have dinner alone instead of eating with the rest of the family; or not to be given any pudding. In that event it was desirable that Papa should not notice:

Thursday, 26th September:

I am much amused by remarking the pains taken by the children, particularly Agnes & Henry, to prevent their Papa observing that they are under punishment. They keep their meat upon their plate till the rest of the party have finished dinner, in order that their inaction during Pudding time may not betray them.

Selina Wright's children also produced some "sayings" which she thought worth mentioning. She wrote to Lady Agnes in December 1836 about her eldest son, John, who was five and a half:

Johnny is writing to Aunt Augusta, he writes <u>letters</u> so much better than <u>copies</u> that I am tempted to let him perform as much as he pleases – his little vanity takes pains when it is for little Aunt to see...

We have such a flood...the Trent is in our field. Johnny came wild with wonder into our room this morning. "Mamma, Papa, the Trent is <u>upset</u>" & then afterwards, when trying to explain the <u>why</u> of the Phenomenon to Henry [4] he said "The Trent was too full, Harry, & so it <u>spilled</u> over" which seemed very expressive...

Little Selina [3 months] grows so plump & smiles so prettily. Bessy [2] walks quite well alone now & Agnes [3] grows more chattery – when we ask her <u>What she is worth</u> Johnny has taught her to make a Curtsey & say "Nothing at all".

The Governess problem

As children grew beyond the toddler stage most well-to-so families found a governess to begin their education. The roles of governess and nanny overlapped. In theory the nanny was responsible for the younger children's welfare and bodily needs, while the governess dealt with the education and social training of the older children.

A baby carriage

Nannies were usually more permanent, serving two or more generations. Governesses tended to move from one family to another after a few years and were usually of a higher social class than nannies. In the early 19th century neither had any "official" qualifications; relatives, friends and acquaintances took the place of advertising or agencies.

At Tissington Hall in February 1825 Lady Agnes was on the look-out for a new governess for the younger children. On 28th she wrote to Sir Henry:

> I have seen a Governess and would give anything for your judgement on the occasion. She is an English Woman, 36 years of age and has been a Governess for fourteen years – she lived last in the Earl of Gosford's Family. She also lived some years with the Yorkshire Dennisons...another Family she lived in is a Lady St.Paul, the sister of Lady Ravensworth & they give her a most excellent character.

> She is a perfect <u>Mistress</u> of Music, teaches French and Italian, writing, Arithmetic, Geography & the Use of the Globes...Mrs Dennison thought very highly of her & the young ladies correspond with her now...

> One of her reasons for leaving Lady Gosford's Family was that she, her Ladyship, is one of the <u>good</u> & she thinks it necessary to have so many books on the subject of Religion, many of which did much more harm than good, in short she seems quite to agree in opinion with you on Religious subjects & thinks it ought not to be made a display of, but to enter into all our everyday actions & conduct. She really appears to me a woman of cultivated mind & good sound sense.

She engaged the Governess, Miss Hackett, in March, having "received from Lady Gosforth a most satisfactory character of her, both in the essentials and Accomplishments". However, in little over a year, Miss Hackett was being replaced by another. Lady Agnes wrote to Sir Henry

> *7th June 1826*
> I have engaged a Governess without consulting you – it is one who has lived three years with Lady Boothby & four years with Lady Mary Sheppard...she teaches Music & Italian perfectly & Lady Boothby says she is very well informed & has numerous excellent

qualifications. I knew no time was to be lost, as they are so soon gone & several people were enquiring about her. She is a Swiss lady.

I hope you will think I have done right. Her salary is a hundred guineas but as she teaches all these things <u>perfectly</u> and is, besides a very superior woman, I think it will be less for her than ninety-two to Miss Hackett.

Then she was anxious for the new governess to start. "I am rather fidgetty as I have not heard again from Lady Boothby. I hope there is no hitch about the Governess".

In 1838 Lady Agnes was once more having governess problems. She told Sir Henry some of her misgivings about the young lady:

> She is very steady & well-looking, without being at all handsome...she had given great satisfaction in the Bishop's family – but then she was only engaged to give instruction in the German Language & Music... She is young-looking for a person of six & twenty... If her French is bad that would make her of no use to Gussy, except for the Music.

D'Ewes Coke mentioned his children's Governess, Miss Burgess, in his Diary on a few occasions:

13th January 1817

> ...to Derby and back to meet Miss Burgess with whom I have been corresponding, as governess to my 4 youngest Children. Her appearance & manners are favourable.

4th March

> Miss Burgess breakfasted with me... When [the children] were gone to bed she sat with me in the Library. From what I have as yet seen of her I like her much – her manner quick & genteel and her appearance sedate.

Little Children

16th March

> In the Evening inspected Miss Burgess's Private Diary, which I
> directed her to keep, of the Children's manners, disposition &
> conduct. It was done much to my satisfaction. They had contested
> with her for the mastery in my absence & had not behaved well in
> general.

By August his admiration for Miss Burgess had waned. He noted, on
an outing with the children on Sunday 31st:

> Walked over Stanton Moor to Stanton & home again, about 2 hours
> in all. I thought Miss B's observations unusually trifling & ignorant.

By 1820 the D'Ewes Coke family had another governess, Miss Mercier,
and also a visiting Drawing Master, Music Master and Dancing Master.
Miss Mercier also proved to be rather disappointing as governess:

Sunday, 27th August:

> All went to Church. Had some sharp conversation with Miss
> Mercier on her extreme neglect of Henry & Richard. It appears they
> do nothing before breakfast & nothing in the afternoon - & they are
> sent out before Eleven in the forenoon to idle as they please. She is
> little more attentive to the girls.

The Little FitzHerberts

The FitzHerbert children enjoyed an idyllic life between babyhood and later childhood, with their parents and elder brothers and sisters all relishing their progress. In 1824 the children at home were: Maria (7), Anthony (6), John (4), Judith (2) and Fanny (7 months). Selina, the eldest child, was seventeen and acted as a governess to the young ones. Augusta did not arrive until 1828. The three older boys were at boarding school.

Selina wrote to her father (then on his way to the West Indies) on 13th June 1824, mentioning the progress of her "pupils"

> Anthony longs to begin his Latin & Johnny plagues sadly & pleases me too; he begs so hard to <u>learn Music</u>. I have promised him if he reads well at 5 years old he shall begin...tho' he longs to run up & down the keys, as his fingers are very supple, he had better wait.

Lady Agnes wrote soon after, reporting:

> Anthony is very nice & attentive & is trying to learn to thread his Grandmama's needles. Judith too is quite charming & has taken her place in the Quadrille, she manages Chaine des Dames delightfully...Maria wishes to write a line. I must give her the pen.

There follows, in inch-high letters: "Dear Papa your affectionate Maria".

An outdoor party

Little Children

On 2nd December Lady Agnes wrote with more news of the children's progress:

> ...all the dear little ones are well, Fanny weaned & quite fat & lazy, and calls the cows & chews for the Cat & grunts for the Pig and is so entertaining & Alas you can not see her...Anthony says he remembers, when he sat upon your knee before Judith was born, you used to talk to him about going to Barbadoes.

Within a fortnight of her writing, the three older boys had come home for Christmas holidays, a great occasion for the little ones. Lady Agnes wrote:

> Alleyne looks happy and is kissing & patting Judith whose little eyes sparkle...dear little Fanny looks very gracious upon William and has walked half the length of the room alone to show off to her brother...

In January 1825 Lady Agnes was again reassuring Sir Henry that the children were all in good health:

> ...dear Maria quite fat and rosy and your little Fanny so pretty and animated and walking about everywhere quite independently, twining in between chairs and tables and laughing when she escapes without a bump or a tumble...little John is taking great pains to learn to write, that he may tell dear Papa how dearly he loves him. Little Judith is as gay as a lark but never forgets her little Prayer for you.

Grandma Beresford with Augusta

Selina

In March Selina wrote, referring to John's progress:

> Johnny improves surprizingly in his Music, he has such an excellent ear & is so fond of it. He knows his notes almost as well as I do; & he is not flat at his sharps & flats; that is our every day joke at the Piano Forte. By June 1827 Fanny was three-and-a-half, and was beginning lessons. Lady Agnes reported to Sir Henry, who was in London.

Maria   Fanny

> ...little Fanny is quite angry, she will not send you her love [because he had gone away again] she says she will not learn her catechism, she "does not want to be gooder".

By November 1832 Augusta was four years old and had taken over the role of toddler from Fanny. Sir Henry was on his second trip to the West Indies when Lady Agnes wrote:

...dear little Gussy is more winning every day...she wishes you would not stay so long, sometimes her little heart quite beats when she talks of you & her little voice trembles, she always sits with me at breakfast.

In July 1834, when Gussy was nearly six, Lady Agnes wrote to Sir Henry in London:

Little Children

...the children are very happy and we walk & read, & garden, and Gussy says "Oh dear, that naughty man to leave me to do all this alone".

When a little more grown-up, and able to write for herself, in large letters, on double-ruled lines, she still showed a complete lack of the formal respect a child was usually meant to show towards parents:

14th January 1835

My dear old Pa

Pray make haste and come to own little Gussy. You must, if you please, bring me a new large doll's head, and neck, and arms, because Mrs Harlow has given me a beautiful doll's bonnet and my poor doll has lost her head. Do not forget your affectionate

Augusta FitzHerbert.

Punishment

Punishment for bad behaviour was rare at Tissington Hall. The only record is one scrap of paper. On one side is written: "Dear Pater, May I

Richard

William

come downstairs? The favour of an answer is required. Alleyne F." On the other side is the reply: "Dear Alleyne, You may come downstairs, you are a good Boy. H.Fitzherbert".

Judith   Lady Agnes

In the D'Ewes Coke family at Brookhill Hall there was a heavy emphasis on punishment. This frequently took the form of being deprived of a meal, or part of a meal. The governess, Miss Burgess, was required to keep a record for the children's father to see.

On 18th January 1818 Richard failed to learn his lesson properly and "lost his Plumb Pudding, Dessert and Wine for his idleness, & being at last threatened with whipping, got thro' it pretty well". A week later he "lost Fish, Plumb Pudding & Dessert". These were not isolated events:

4th March
> [Richard] has had only Broth & Bread for his dinner.

5th March
> Miss Agnes...has been deprived of her pudding. Master Richard has had a scanty dinner of cold meat and sent early to bed after a Supper of bread alone.

In May, on 3rd, 6th and 13th Richard and some of the other children "lost their pudding". Sometimes their suppertime milk was stopped, as on 27th March. "The two young gentlemen have been deprived of their milk at supper, as a punishment for misconduct during play-hours".

The practice of using food in this way sometimes actually led the children into bad behaviour, through perceived, or actual hunger. It was a rule that "no one shall have their breakfast till two lessons are learnt by each". Friday, 13th February 1818 was an unlucky day for Richard, who:

> ...contrived to slip into the Store room, and eat part of his, unobserved, before anyone else went into the room and before he had even attempted his lesson. This piece of generalship was discovered and punished by the forfeiture of the remainder.

Richard, however, continued to be very disobedient, or very hungry:

Tuesday, 17th February

> Miss Agnes was detained by an imperfect lesson from going to breakfast with her companions. When she went shortly after, she found the breakfast things removed and Mary Goodall [the Maid] told her all the basins were empty. I had left Richard a few minutes before, in the room alone, and had observed a full basin. I taxed him with having eaten it, which he denied so quietly, unblushingly, and with a face of such perfect innocence, that I sent for the servant, thinking there must be some mistake.

But no – Richard had been unable to resist an unguarded bowl of porridge. Miss Burgess added, "I have punished him severely, tho' I fear inadequately".

Fanny FitzHerbert and Augusta   Sir Henry Fitz Herbert

In April 1817 D'Ewes Coke had written a complaint to his elder sons' schoolmaster about the danger of "cuffing" boys, but he seems to have condoned Miss Burgess' habit of boxing the ears of his younger children. He read the following in her "Diary":

Friday, 6th February

> Miss Agnes...cannot yet pursue the strait forward path of truth. She has had her ears well boxed today for an offence of this kind.

Sunday, 5th April

> Master Richard has had his ears boxed for his impudent disobedience [in going into the Drawing Room where there were some visitors]. I followed him and boxed his ears in the room before the ladies.

Wednesday, 22nd April

> Masters H. & R. have had their ears boxed, and sent early to bed for playing with fire and other improper conduct.

Sending to bed early, withholding food, and boxing ears did not exhaust the repertoire of punishment; the whip, cane, or stick was always to hand:

Little Children

Monday, 23rd February

The day was begun by my young friends creating a little riot in their bedrooms, for which I gave each of them two or three cuts with a little switch which I keep in the school room.

Wednesday, 3rd June

Master Henry and Richard have been confined during an hour of their playtime for going into the garden without leave, and taking some roots up. I flogged Richard because he said (when I met him with a strawberry plant in his hand) that the Gardener had given it to him [but] the Gardener had not seen them.

By August Miss Burgess' patience had worn away. She warned Richard that if his behaviour did not improve "either I would chastise him severely or beg his Papa to do it". A few days later she wrote, "I have this morning given Richard a smart flogging". Five-year-old Richard, however, seemed ready to test her resolution:

Tuesday, 4th August

I assured my friend Richard yesterday that I had begun with him determined to flog him every day till he learnt his lessons with less trouble and interruption to me...he seems resolved to ascertain how far I can keep my word; it was not till he had felt the cane that he began his morning's tasks.

Occasionally, one's sympathies come close to lying with the governess. The two small boys had a fascination with the garden pond. In March Richard got "completely wet to the skin" through ladling water out of the pond. In June Henry and Richard were sent to bed for going into the pond wearing their shoes and stockings. In July, again, "The two young Gents amused themselves by walking into the pond". And again:

12th August

Master Richard has amused himself both last evening and this, by sitting on the side of the pond and putting his feet in the water, stockings & shoes inclusive.

Miss Burgess' Diary sheds some light on how much the children were expected to know intuitively about correct behaviour. In April 1818 Agnes was eight. Her governess wrote: "[Her] mind is still deficient of that sense of duty which at her age we may reasonably expect to begin to shew itself". In June Agnes, now just nine, exhibited this "deficiency" in the following incident.

> Miss Agnes was sent to bed early in the evening in great disgrace...She went out of doors with the rest after supper. I followed them rather earlier than was expected and found Miss A. amongst a large party of Men who were shaking the carpets, lolling against the wall in conversation with the Gardener. I have often severely reproved her & not infrequently boxed her ears for her familiarity with the Men Servants. To see her one in such a party both shocked and surprised me.

Liberty days

A very different picture of life at home with a governess is given by Elizabeth Mosley of Holbrook, born in 1798. She wrote her childhood memories down in 1879.

She was one of six children, five girls and one boy. Her mother taught them French and her father taught the older children writing, but he tended to let his attention wander, and to begin reading his own books instead of teaching the children:

> My mother left us all in the room with him one day, & we pushed everything we could get to the door. When she came back she could not get in, & it was very long before she could rouse my father to see what was going on.
>
> At that time servants & workmen used to sing at their work. We learnt "The Galley Slave" from Wigley the Carpenter; "A Rose Tree in Full Bearing" from the Laundry Maid; "Mary's Dream" from a Nurse...We were not taught them but caught them by the ear.

Little Children

Elizabeth recalled a childhood fancy which involved a beggar woman who called at the house every Christmas:

> ...she used to sing "God bless you noble Master, and Mistress also and all the little children that round the table go". And we had a round table in the breakfast room & used to run round it – so we thought the couplet referred to that.

When their mother died their father let nurses and servants look after them until Charlotte, the eldest girl, was seven. Then she, Maria (6) and Elizabeth herself (5) were sent to a boarding school in Wirksworth, where they stayed for two years. Then her father and most of the children went to live in another home near Tutbury, leaving Maria and Elizabeth living with two aunts at Holbrook:

> Those were liberty days. No lessons & Nanny Barker to pet us. Sometimes she would give us thick Oat Cakes with our tea, & so thickly buttered that the butter would trickle down our bare arms to the elbows. We were out a great deal, either at play or in mischief. Maria made great pets of the cows. We had not even to go to Chapel.

This lasted only a few months and then they joined their father and the rest of the family in the new house at Barton Blount. Here they had a Governess, Miss Cook:

> We had <u>no</u> books but lesson books...We were well grounded in all History, Geography, Chronology, Arithmetic, etc...Once a fortnight a Music Master came from Buxton, name, Thomas Yates, irreverently called by my Father "Tinkling Tommy"...The dancing master, Mr. Lascelles, came from Nottingham, gave us a whole day...and staid the night.

Like many other children of the time they each had "little gardens in borders round a little plot of grass", and their father's four principal tenant farmers each invited them for tea once a year. "Then we had the range of farm buildings for hide-and-seek, and saw the cheese made, etc".

When Elizabeth was about thirteen, their relatives insisted that Miss Cook should go, and that their father should send them to a proper school. To their delight, the Governess left in the early summer, weeks before any schooling could be arranged.

We enjoyed some weeks of entire liberty...to play out of doors much of the day...and to read, draw, & play on the piano after our several tastes. [We] used to go about our fields with leaping poles [and spoilt] a set of very valuable pointer puppies, taking them out in our rambles armed with dog-whips, which we never used, and dog whistles which were seldom idle.

Eventually their father's gamekeepers complained and that pastime had to stop. In August the girls were sent to local schools, and the next year Elizabeth and Maria were packed off to a finishing school in Doncaster.

Nannies

The FitzHerbert Nanny, Mrs Hardy, occupied a position almost as one of the family. When Lady Agnes was staying at Farleigh she often wrote, telling her family news. In June 1831she wrote to Mrs Hardy about Selina's baby.

> ...we have got a very nice wet nurse for the dear little baby & he thrives well...[Selina] has had a cup of milk porridge made exactly after your manner – she wished you could have made it her yourself.

The next day she added directions for the painting of various rooms in the Hall while the family were away, including "the outside of the cistern in the water closet". In May 1835 Lady Agnes wrote about the re-covering of "sofas, armed chairs, etc", and asked, "Pray let me know if the gentleman has been to repair the Piano Forte in the Schoolroom".

Mrs Hardy was clearly in charge when the family were away, and Lady Agnes was apologetic about asking her to supervise. She wrote, "I am very troublesome to you, but I know you have a pleasure in obliging me".

Lady Agnes wrote, telling her about her mother's (Mrs Beresford's) death in July 1833, and the children often wrote to their nanny, throughout their lives. Selina wrote to "Dearest Nanny" in April 1830, saying how they all miss her:

> ...now I want...to sneak into the old nursery corner at your tea time to have a cup of tea with you & chat to comfort me...My little Brothers & Sisters all desire their best love to you & a great many kisses.

Judith (13) wrote in 1835 to tell her how she had "a dip in the sea".

William wrote to tell her at length about the birth of his first child, and Selina kept her informed about her children, who also wrote.

Selina's daughter Agnes (12) wrote in 1845 sending "these Muffitees...I hope you will like them; Mamma says...they will wear better than any other colour".

Very little survives of Mrs Hardy's own thoughts. A couple of her remarks do shed some light on her personality. In February 1825 Lady Agnes wrote to Sir Henry who had just arrived in Barbados:

> I am now a great deal engaged nursing poor Nanny who has had a most severe attack of Cholera Morbus...Dr. Sims has been most attentive...I must say a word of dear little Johnny [4], Nanny said, when we were debating who he should sleep with, the night she was so ill, "Oh! Anybody will like him, he is as soft as a mole".

In the previous December, when Sir Henry was sailing to Barbados, a neighbour, Mrs Bainbridge, sent Lady Agnes a message saying not to complain, "but think of her poor Tom" who had gone to sea, with some

PRACTICE.

convicts for Botany Bay. Nanny's outraged comment was that "her Tom was not the father of nine children".

How fortunate the young FitzHerberts were may be judged by a brief reference to another Derbyshire Nanny of the 1850s, described by Lord Curzon of Kedleston Hall. From the age of five, as well as beatings with slippers and hair-brushes, he and his siblings were made to walk through the grounds and around the village, wearing large notices indicating their current sins and shortcomings – LIAR SNEAK COWARD, etc. Their parents were apparently unaware or unconcerned at the nanny, Miss Paraman's methods of child care.

The Pinafore Saga

One of the milestones that a little boy passed at the age of four or five was the transition from baby clothes or petticoats to trousers or breeches. He would still wear a pinafore to protect his clothes, but he was expected to be able to dress himself and tie the strings of his pinafore in a bow, at the back. The story of Richard D'Ewes Coke is told in the Diary or Log Book which the Governess had to keep,in January 1818:

Saturday, 3rd
> Richard measured for Boys' Clothes, having accomplished the tying his own Pinafore.

His fifth birthday was coming on 12th February. He tried on his new clothes on 6th January. Everything seemed to be going well – but not for long.

Wednesday, 7th
> Richard totally unable to tie his Pinafore, Mary Goodall [the Maid] having done it for him for 2 or 3 days, without my knowledge. His rabbit at Dinner taken away, & himself threatened to be put into petticoats again.

Thursday, 8th
> Richard had his ears pulled for prevaricating about the tying of his pinafore.

Friday 9th

> Richard tied a good double bow in his Pinafore & on my expressing doubts of his doing it, he untied it again to prove he <u>could</u> do it. The second attempt failed, & he produced only a single bow – gave him 6d for his double bow.

Sunday, 11th

> The tying of Richard's pinafore is a constant subject of vigilance...The Children & Servants are peremptorily forbidden to assist him, & he is allowed no Breakfast, Dinner, or Supper, till he produces a double & single Bow in the Strings. This he now regularly does.

But this was not the end...

Saturday, 17th

> Richard nearly lost his breakfast by not tying his Pinafore. After being put in a corner in my room for some time, he produced a double bow.

Two days later he was still having difficulty, and Miss Burgess thought of a way to help him, by getting him to tie the bow in front, but with his eyes shut. It seemed to work! Or so she thought...

Tuesday, 20th

> Put a bandage over Richard's eyes, & then he failed in tying his pinafore, from which it is evident, he <u>peeped</u> yesterday, & played a trick on me.

Thursday, 22nd

> Richard appears to understand the method of tying a Bow, at last.

But the final mention of Richard's pinafore came a week later:

Thursday, 29th

> Richard full half an hour tying his Pinafore.

A fortnight later, on 12th February, Richard faced another milestone. It was his fifth birthday. The entry for the day reads:

> Richard has today begun to use the pen & ink...His beginning is not very promising.

Games, Hobbies and Holidays

I am going to have some stuff or another over it...because I am going to keep big beetles &c in it which would get out...I shall bring back an enormous number of newts for I want them to breed at home – I shall turn them into the ponds.

Richard Turbutt reassuring his mother about his planned aquarium, 1867.

Walks

The simplest (and usually the most boring) pastime for children was walking. This is nowhere more aptly illustrated than in D'Ewes Coke's Diary for 1817:

Wednesday, 2nd April
> Walked with the Children to the Wharf & shewed them all the Coalpit, Railway, &c.

Thursday, 3rd April
> Walked with the Children to Bole Hill to gather violets; from there to Langton.

Wednesday, 25th June
> Walked with all the Children to the Rocking Stones at Birchover, & was much fatigued by it, having allowed too little time for the walk, & they afforded no conversation whatever.

W/ TANNER

Games, Hobbies and Holidays

A stage further in turning children against walks was to make it an occasion for rules and punishments, as the D'Ewes Coke governess shows in her Diary:

Saturday, 18th September 1818

> I have made it a constant regulation...that no one shall eat anything they gather in the hedges without first showing it to me. If they gather Blackberries they bring them to me; if thoroughly ripe I permit them to eat a very few. In our walk today Miss Agnes [9] was sent back to shut a gate...we observed her eating Blackberries the whole of the way back to the gate...I said "Agnes, you know I have a particular objection to your eating blackberries". She unhesitatingly answered, "I have not eaten one, Madam". I gave her a long hymn to learn...and suffered no one to speak to her during the evening.

Eight-year-old William Turbutt wrote to his Mama on 27th February 1861, telling her of a much more pleasant experience:

> I had a nice walk yesterday after you were gone, as the sun shone so brightly, and in passing the lodge, Mrs. Spencer asked me whether I liked a few eggs for tea & I said yes, so she gave me six little bantom eggs.

The FitzHerbert children were usually occupied in more interesting things than mere walking. A rare reference to a walk comes in a letter to Sir Henry (then in Barbados) in January 1825 from Rev. William Alderson, an elderly family friend: "Selina, William and Dick made Mrs.A and Myself walk to very summit of Thorpe Cloud on Wednesday last".

Soon after, Sir Henry had a letter from Selina telling the same story rather more colourfully:

> Mr & Mrs Alderson spent a few days with us...we walked one day with them to the top of Thorpe Cloud! & Mr. A. told us how often he had climbed up to its summit &c, &c. You would have been much amused to have seen us clambering up the opposite hill in a strong wind, Mr. A. first, & one behind the other, each holding fast by the coat of the former. Ilam looked quite enchanting.

Gardens

Most children, where circumstances allowed, were given their own patch of garden to look after. This could be very satisfying, but only in the growing season, and during dry weather. As Anthony FitzHerbert wrote from Tissington to his Dear Mama in July 1788: "We have very little to amuse us hear, the weather is so bad that we cant get to the Garden". Two years later he wrote in March to say: "We have begun to make a Gardin and intend to get some Peas and Radish seed. The weather has been remarkable fine..." By the end of April, his brother George was able to report that "the Peas and Radishes are come up very well".

The D'Ewes Cokes had gardens also, but as one might expect, they were also used as a means of punishment. In 1818 the governess recorded, referring to Agnes' lessons:

Thursday, 13th August

> ...quite imperfect...I have told her that she shall never again go to her Garden excepting she repeats her lessons perfectly and that if she persists her present negligence I will take it from her and give it to some one more worthy.

Saturday, 15th August

> ...lessons indifferently said...She was not allowed to go to her Garden. This is a punishment which she seems to think a good deal about.

The Turbutt boys in the early 1860s had gardens at home as well as at school in Brighton. Willie frequently mentioned plants. "Gardener gave me some heath to plant in my rockery. I have a little creeper in a pot in the nursery". "Will you ask gardener to make our gardens tidy before we come home?"

If the FitzHerberts had gardens there is very little mention of them in their letters. Selina, however, was interested in flowers, and a couple of her letters are worth quoting, as much for her style as for the content. It is only fair to point out that she was eighteen at the time – though still a child by the standards of the period.

The first letter touches on a number of subjects – Selina did not make a distinction between flowers and pets as we eavesdroppers do. Her letter was intended to entertain her Dearest Papa, who was then, in December 1824, on his way to the West Indies:

> Mama has told you about my room; it was to have been papered with an elegant paper, birds being depicted thereon & the border, sugar canes. The choice shewed our taste for it turned out so extremely dear that in despair we were forced to give up; however, to console ourselves for the disappointment my dear Grandmama & I are to go halves in a live piping Bullfinch...I shall make [him] learn to pipe your favourites.
>
> Don't you laugh at the idea of my pet Dormouse at Farleigh & a pet piping bird at T..., besides that, I am coaxing a great cat, for g! sake [as well as] the usual complements of Dogs & puppies, Hens, chickens & children; robbin redbreasts during the snow & my sweet Piggy Wiggy. All these are my dumb beasts.
>
> Then, you know, I have the geraniums, roses, &c., and my beautiful hyacinths which I shall carry with us to Town...we can take them very easily...
>
> Yr very affte. Daughter SF
>
> I look very nice in my new green gown, your present; that is, it looks most beautiful.

A month later Selina wrote to say how she intended to take her hyacinths to London. In 1825 they were quite a novelty. She referred to them as "my pets". The white and the blue ones were beginning to show their colours and they were quite tall. They could easily have been broken on the journey, but Selina was resourceful:

> The mode of conveyance is either in the Phaeton Hood or on my knees & the instrument a very convenient little basket made to my order, something resembling a bottle-basket with the proper number of holes & as compact as possible.

Pets

More conventional pets were mentioned in 1791 by Henry in a letter to his mother. "Our little cats are well and we are as fond of them as ever". His brother George added, "Little Wimsey I think is going to have some kittens, which makes us very happy. The Peacocks and Hen are very well but we don't hear of any Eggs she has laid".

In the next generation, Selina mentioned hens in October 1820: "The five chickens are well...Twilight is very broody, Bastia lays very well indeed". In 1821, Richard, at Charterhouse School, wrote to his mother: "I hope we shall see you on Saturday & you will tell us all about the hens, dogs, horses, cows &c". Soon after William wrote home to Sir Henry:

> Pray ask Selina to send us a very particular account of the hens...by their names and the chickens by their colours and genders.

Disaster!

Schoolboys of eleven and thirteen enquiring anxiously about hens? A letter written by Richard to his father the following January sheds some light on the matter:

> We have had no eggs from the Polands yet, but the other hens lay very well. We have made up a shilling's worth.

The business of the hens becomes steadily clearer each year. In February 1822, Richard, at school, wrote to his father:

> I suppose we have got a little profit by the hens now, although eggs are so cheap. I am glad so many hens lay as you told me in your last letter.

In 1823 William enquired about a new hennery being built. Richard, at school, wrote to Alleyne, at home:

> I suppose you...go up with Selina to help feed the hens. Do they lay now?

A few years later it was Alleyne, away at school, who was writing to Anthony:

How are the hens now? I suppose you now go out and see about them with Maria & Johnny & Judith every morning. Do they lay well? No chickens yet, I suppose? Pray write soon and tell me all about them.

In 1827 Alleyne wrote asking Anthony to "Tell Selina that eggs have got us about 14s-7d". In 1833, not yet quite 13, Anthony was taking an active part. He told his father:

I bought such a very nice hen at Bentley the other day for eighteen pence. It is a white one with brown spots on it and we call it Speckle. It has not begun to lay yet.

How the selling of the eggs was done, and how the profits were shared, is unclear, but all the children gained experience of husbandry, a sense of responsibility, and *an interest* in poultry. Anthony used a very apposite term in a letter from Harrow to Sir Henry in March 1834:

I long to see our new present, the little Cock, which I hope The Firm expressed their most dutiful thanks for.

Hens were not the only pets at Tissington Hall. In August 1827 Anthony referred to foals, five hives of bees, and ferrets. Alleyne gave him instruction about the latter..."keep them quite dry and warm with plenty of straw for their beds". The ferrets, like the hens, were not just pets. They discouraged rats and could be used for catching rabbits. Cats were kept mainly to catch mice and rats, but a cat might also be someone's particular pet. In July 1842 Sir Henry wrote home to Lady Agnes, on behalf of Augusta, then thirteen. The letter imitates Gussy's imperious style:

Miss Augusta is much afraid that they will destroy her Stable Cat for killing some chickens; but she begs that I will request you to see Dick Marsh immediately, and desire him to feed the Cat regularly every day, as she thinks that it may be from want of food that she has killed the chickens.

Augusta also had a more unusual pet, a parrot, perhaps a present from the West Indies, which seems not to have been everybody's favourite. Selina mentioned its demise, writing from her own home at Lamcote in 1836:

So Gussy's poor poll is no more – a happy release, if not for itself, for its hearers I should think. She should have it stuffed au naturel, with its head on one side, looking vicious.

In 1863, William Turbutt was more interested in Nature Study than in more usual pets. While he was away at school the governess, Miss Rumelin, had the job of looking after things, with frequent reminders from William:

March

> Will you ask Miss Rumelin how my aquarium is getting on and if the water is almost dried up?

September

> Will you tell me how my aquarium is getting on and if it has not got enough water in it will you put some more in it? And will you also ask Miss Rumelin how my ferns are getting on?

November

> Will you give my love to Miss Rumelin and ask her [whether] my ferns are alive still?

He had other interests too. In October he wrote to his mother: "Will you tell me how the little bird is getting on and whether it is quite well? Will you ask Miss Rumelin whether my catirpiller is alive still?" And again, later, "Will you tell me next time you write how the little bird is getting on?"

The little bird was probably either a bullfinch or a siskin, which were commonly kept as pets. Selina FitzHerbert and her Grandmama bought a bullfinch in 1824. George Strutt sent a "siskine" home from Harrow for Adela in 1892 – "the bird will be 2s-6d and postage a little more". The household encyclopaedia, "Enquire Within", of 1871 gave advice on keeping bullfinches (and also blackbirds, thrushes, linnets and skylarks). It suggested that they might be given "a grain or two of rice steeped in Canary Wine, when teaching them to pipe, as a reward for the progress they make".

The all-too-likely outcome of a child's interest in birds in the 19th century is shown in Richard Turbutt's request to his father in June 1865:

> Will you ask Keeper to shoot every very rare bird that he sees and if you think that I should like to have it stuffed, will you do so?

By 1867 when the boys were at Harrow, Richard had become seriously interested in pond life. He wrote to Dear Mama on 25th April:

> I have got two large water beetles (Dystici marginales) male and female. I am going to get a large square aquarium as my other is much too small, for I shall bring back all sorts of things with me:- The two large water beetles that I have now, newts 6 inches long, sticklebacks, small water beetles, boatmen &c. and I shall put in minnows and young carp at home, so I wish you could send me the address of the aquarium man at Derby & I shall write for a list.

On 2nd May he wrote again about the aquarium:

> I am also going to have some stuff or other over it...because I am going to keep big beetles &c. in it which would get out...I shall bring back an enormous number of newts for I want them to breed at home.

And he added, picturing his mother's reaction, perhaps: "I shall turn them into the ponds". On 8th May he informed her: "You can get large aquariums, about two feet each way for 35s". And on 16th: "Try & find out about an aquarium as soon as possible".

Another letter contained the sad news that "My male Dysticus Marginalis died a day or two ago so I have pinned it out in my collection".

His mother seems to have shared his enthusiasm. In a later letter he tells her "The insect you caught is possibly a water spider". And in June 1872, in his final year at Harrow, he wrote, "I wish I was with you at Scarborough...If I was with you we might set up a sea-water aquarium".

George Strutt made few references in his letters to pets or other pastimes which he enjoyed at home, and those few are not very informative:

23rd February 1891

> I should think [it] will be best to sell the pigeons to the man in Derby please sell about 2 best pair of fantails, 1 pair of Jacobins and keep as many fliers as you want for eating. I am very glad that the new pony goes well in the donkey cart.

In 1895 there is an annoyingly short reference to a new pastime, not available to the D'Ewes Cokes or the FitzHerberts earlier in the 19th century: "I expect Isabel & Adela like cycling awfully".

More active pastimes for older children included the familiar rural trio of hunting, shooting and fishing.

Shooting

Shooting was not as popular in the early 19th century as it became later, when loading and firing sporting guns became simpler and quicker. A terse entry in D'Ewes Coke's Diary for 1820 reads: "Monday 17th January. Sent D'Ewes & William shooting". In 1829 Anthony FitzHerbert wrote home: "Alleyne...wishes to know whether he might shoot rooks next holidays, as Mr. Tolhurst [a master at Charterhouse] has got a very nice little gun, and said he would sell it to Alleyne for £2...We both shot a little when we were at Farleigh the Holidays before last".

Fishing

Fishing was a more usual and safer sport for children. There are a few brief references in the D'Ewes Coke letters and an entry in the Diary in August 1820: "Bought some Fishing Rods for Edward, Henry & Richard".

Maria FitzHerbert (11) wrote from Farleigh to her Papa:

7th June 1827

We wish Aunt Fanny could come & fish with us now the weather will soon be warmer & the fish will bite. I do not know whether I shall like fishing much because I have never yet tried.

The following year Alleyne (13) and Anthony (10) presented their father with a note proposing an original scheme. In it they:

...humbly petition the favor of a small sum of money to be laid out in fishing tackle &c. Subscriptions of two pounds a year, to be paid quarterly, will entitle any person to the use of the Tackle bought by such subscription; & any such subscriber will be admitted as a

member to the Society. If a person does not wish to subscribe, any donation will be thankfully received.N.B. Ae., & Ay., FitzHerbert wish it to be secret at present.

We may not be far wrong in supposing that the donation was expected to come from Sir Henry.

Alleyne was a very keen angler. In 1828 he wrote home hoping that William Johnson would teach him fly-fishing for "the Dear little trout in the Dear little Dove". William Johnson was an expert. In 1832 Selina's father-in-law wrote to Sir Henry asking if he could get William to make him "a few of the most likely killing flies for grayling" as he was bringing a fishing party to Dovedale.

Hunting

Hunting was an extension of riding, which was an accomplishment rather than a pastime in itself. Like 20th century children learning to ride a bicycle, children in the 18th and 19th centuries, if they could, learned to ride a donkey or a pony (owned, hired or borrowed) and later graduated to a horse. George FitzHerbert wrote to his mother from Tissington:

17th March 1791
> I had a very nice ride to Bradbourne to day and when I come home Henry and Fanny gets a ride on Billy round the yard and they like it as well as me.

The following week he wrote:

> I had a very good ride to Dovedale yesterday, it was exceedingly fine and pleasant and Brother Henry accompany'd me there. He rode before Joseph... [sitting in front of Joseph, the groom].

Of the next generation (brother Henry's children) the eldest boy, William, first mentioned hunting in a letter in 1824, when he was sixteen:

Wednesday, 15th December
> ...we had not very good sport. I rode a poney Mr. Fletcher lent me but it had not a very good idea of leaping...[Next Friday] Col. Wilson intends to hunt a bag fox, & throws off at Hanging Bridge...

His next letter brings out the excitement of the cross-country gallop, and the risks involved, but also the need to reassure his father who was on his way to the West Indies:

18th December 1824

...I was riding a two-year-old...I was capsized twice, but I did not light on my head & if I had it would not have killed me as it was quite boggy where I fell...very hard galloping over a good deal of ploughed ground...Dick ejected two or three times but not hurt; both of us in at the death...

[Richard added] Had a capital day's sport...from near Ashbourne almost to Kedleston and then back again to Flower Lilley, the seat of Mr. Crompton who entertained us all with bread and cheese.

What's in the basket?

Games, Hobbies and Holidays

Cricket and other outdoor pastimes

Cricket was well established in 1791, though often played by children to variable rules by teams of variable numbers. In March of that year George FitzHerbert wrote to his mother in London asking if she could bring him back a cricket ball, adding "Sukey knows what I mean, and Brother Anthony would be very glad of one too, as we cannot get one at Ashbourne".

A generation later, Richard was looking forward to "What fine games at cricket we will have next holidays". In 1824 the boys, going to Harrogate where the rest of the family would meet them, wrote, "Pray bring the largest & the hardest of the cricket balls from Tissington". At ten, Maria was allowed, or persuaded, to make up a side. She wrote from Farleigh to Sir Henry in May 1827, telling him proudly, "I know how to play criket now & the Dean [of Rochester] comes and plays with us every evening".

An outdoor amusement not requiring more than one child was kites. A rare reference occurs in September 1829 when Lady Agnes wrote to Sir Henry about Anthony, who had been ill. "He has been a dear, good fellow, amusing himself making Kites".

Twenty years on, the baby Gussy, now grown up, was writing to her father about her own children, and the common fate of kites:

26th April 1849

> Anthony & little Billy have been very busy making a kite, they flew it a few days ago & it went up beautifully far above the Avenue trees, but unluckily the string broke, being too thin, & the poor kite was rather damaged by its fall.

Swimming in a river or pond is mentioned occasionally, and briefly. It was a way of cooling off in very hot weather rather than a popular sport, and, of course, for boys only. The young D'Ewes Cokes learned to swim when they were pupils at Mr Hodgson's in Bakewell in 1818. Typically, their father used the occasion to deliver a short lecture.

19th July 1818

> My Dear D'Ewes,
> I am very glad to hear you & William can really swim. If you can swim round the Bath, you will soon feel confidence enough to

swim across the pond here. But, I would never wish you, wantonly, to go into deep water. The use of swimming is to save yourself, or others, if you get into deep water against your will.

Indoor pastimes

Battledore-and-shuttlecock was safer for ornaments than bat-and-ball, but it was usually played by younger children, and occasioned fewer references in letters and diaries. One, in January 1838, was made by Lady Agnes in a letter to Sir Henry. "Gussy has kept up with Fitz [her nephew] the shuttlecock 91 times!!!!!" Augusta herself wrote a few days later claiming that "Fitz and me have kept up to 107, and he sent me a very good one for the next but I was so tired that I hit it into the curtain".

In December 1860 William Turbutt wrote to his Mama: "We had a game of battle door & shuttlecock yesterday & in the evening I built with my bricks". A slightly later version of the game mentioned by Richard was "battledoor & shuttlecook".

In 1862 Richard wrote about other pastimes:

12 April

My dear Mama

You promised to bring me something when you come home. Would you buy me a little brass cannon to shoot with?...We have had some nice games of lotto. I won the game many times. Miss Rumelin calls the numbers out in German.

Girls, of course, had dolls, which occasionally suffered from the well-meaning intentions of their owners. The following plea came from Tissington Hall by the hand of George FitzHerbert, in 1791:

15th April

Dear Mama

...Fanny will be glad of a new hat. And Doll would be glad of a new pair of Arms as F[anny] would set her hands to rights [and] has broke off all the fingers that remained on that hand.

A hundred years later, Adela Strutt, on holiday in Buxton, was less than happy about another doll (and about life in general):

Games, Hobbies and Holidays

6th March 1891

My dear Muddie

...We went to Millers Dail & then we walked through She Dail & we lost our way & then after a long time we reached the carrage...We have got a doll for Daisy. Aunt Coocoo paid 1s9d, Isabel 1s and I had to pay 1s. It is a Japernise doll & not at all pritty.

Needlework of some sort was another occupation for girls. It began as a learning process and, hopefully, became an enjoyable pastime. Not invariably so, however. The D'Ewes Coke Governess was not very happy about the progress Agnes was making in 1818:

Saturday, 25th April

The remarks I made yesterday respecting Miss A's negligence at her lessons are alike applicable to her at her needle work. She does not sew by any means so well as Emma. She sits staring about her half the time.

Some of the FitzHerbert girls were more enthusiastic. In 1829 Anthony was hoping to get a red and brown purse which Maria had promised to make for him. In December 1832 Maria was finishing a screen "...the subject is the portrait of our little cat on a red cushion".

In 1834 Judith wrote to her mother about a near disaster which befell herself and Fanny while on a visit to relatives at Somersall:

7th October

We came here the greatest beggars imaginable, for when we brought out our work we found we had one thimble between us, one needle, and one skein of Lambswool to work a pair of slippers. However, by our good Cousins contrivance we are quite set up and working something very flash...

Stamp collecting became a hobby as more countries followed the lead of Britain's Penny Post of 1840. The Turbutt boys had begun before they went away to school, and continued there. In February 1864 Richard wrote to say they had bought a stamp album, and asking his mother to bring "the two little books which we put them in – they are in the drawers". Other letters home asked: "Will you collect some stamps and send them to me when you write?"; "Will you send me some foreigne stamps?". And (an advantage of having a German

Governess), "Will you ask Miss Rumelin whether she can send me some German stamps?"

George Strutt, at Prep School in Elstree in 1891, seems to have shared the hobby with his sister Isabel. "Pleas thank Isabel for the stamps she sent me & tell her I have got 564 different ones in the book". "Please tell Isabel I am keeping the stamp book clean and have got a lot more rare stamps".

Winter evenings

Long evenings called for pastimes that children of different ages could join in, including music, dancing and card-games. The FitzHerberts of the 1820s and 30s, with a large family and a father on occasions away from home, provide the most information on these activities. A letter from Selina to her father in London is worth quoting at length:

> 21st January 1829
>
> My Dear Papa,
>
> Now you are gone I have thought as usual of another little commission for you – if you would be so kind as to bring me the Tyrolese set of Quadrilles. I should think they would sell them at Birchall's. I believe that is not quite the right title but all music sellers will propably know what you mean. We had a grand Quadrille last night – indeed we were dancing all day long...
>
> Believe me Ever my dearest Papa
>
> Your dutiful & affecte Daughter
>
> S.FitzHerbert

A letter from Lady Agnes explained further:

> ...in the evening they danced for more than 2 hours as happily as if all the world had been there to admire them. We finished the Evening with a round at Loo...

Lady Agnes described a winter's evening to Sir Henry in 1824 when he was on his way to the West Indies. It was New Year's Eve, and the two older boys had been invited to a Ball at Stoke by Richard Arkwright, but the arrangements fell through:

> I was determined to make the evening as agreable as I could, and I have been so noble as to make a handsome pool at Commerce &

dear Alleyne has just been the Victor - & the cheering has been not
a little noisy...there is not a shadow of discontent about the Ball and
dear William has been dancing as gay as possible & as happy, with
little Judith.

In January she wrote again, mentioning that Maria and Richard were
improving at dancing and that Alleyne (who was intended for the
Church) had won two pools at Commerce: "We tell him that will not do
for a Bishop".

On Sir Henry's visits to London he was regularly being asked to buy
sheet music. In January 1834 it was "a Duet of Rossini's...price 6s sold
at Birchall's & also the Fall of Paris". In January 1835 Lady Agnes wrote:
"...the Girls send best love and a list of Music you must really bring
everything as they are quite at a stand...they would rather have it than
any fineries".

As each member of the family got older they joined in the dancing,
music and games. In January 1838 Lady Agnes told Sir Henry that they
had been playing Commerce early in the evening so that Gussy (9)
could join in: "...she was most amusing, never would let a creature see
her hand, & manoeuvred admirably".

Simpler pastimes

Joseph Strutt (not one of the Belper family) compiled a book in 1801 entitled *The Sports and Pastimes of the People of England*. It was much enlarged in 1903 by J. C. Cox, who updated it and gave it somewhat of a Derbyshire bias.

Most of the children's games required no special equipment at all. They included hide and seek; chasing and catching games like Hunting the Hare or Prisoners' Base; games of physical strength or skill such as Leap-Frog, and hopping on one foot, trying to knock each other off balance. Activities such as swimming in summer and sliding on the ice in winter likewise needed no cash outlay. For "Horses" a child could use a stick instead of a specially made hobby-horse. For skipping, poor children could use a piece of rope too short for any serious purpose. Games of Hopscotch or Ducks-and- Drakes (or skimmers) only needed some suitable stones. Whipping tops and hoops could be home-made, with some help from the village carpenter perhaps. Kites were another possibility.

Cats and dogs were rarely just pets; most had a serious role in pest control (or in poaching). Joseph Strutt also mentioned "sporting with insects". Beetles and similar small creatures could be caught and made to "race" each other. Flying insects were sometimes tethered or caged – a basketwork cage was not very expensive or difficult to make. Birds-nesting was a seasonal pastime, but it required a sharp eye and plenty of leisure time. This was not so readily available for poor children as

one might imagine. Even if there were no cotton mills or coal mines in an area, the children of the poor worked from the age of seven or younger, helping their parents or earning a few pence from a farmer or other employer.

Books

Very few suitably interesting books were available for children in the early 19th century. In 1819 the FitzHerbert boys were making the best of Oriental Field Sports – "it tells all about hunting tigers and wild boars in India", and Mavor's Voyages through Arabia. In 1824 William was reading The Travels of Mungo Park and went on to Mungo Park's second expedition into the interior of Africa. Alleyne had Guy Mannering, and went on to read A History of Scotland, while William tried Southey's Life of Nelson. These books were all borrowed from the Charterhouse library.

It was well into the 19th century before story books specially written for children made their appearance. Ballantyne's Coral Island and Thomas Hughes' Tom Brown's Schooldays both came out in 1857. Treasure Island was not published until 1883. Harold FitzHerbert wrote to his Aunt Judith in 1875: "I am reading a nice book called Percival Keene, it is by Captain Marryat".

In the 1890s George Strutt had a very wide choice of reading, from The Old Curiosity Shop to The Right of a Conquest and The Iron Pirate, which he described as "awfully exciting". He also had what earlier generations of Derbyshire schoolboys would have loved – The Boy's Own Paper, first published in 1879, price one penny. His letters home are full of reminders for it to be sent to him, and assurances: "I got my boys own paper this morning".

The FitzHerberts had a family custom of reading books or plays aloud on winter evenings. Looking forward to Christmas holidays in December 1822 Richard wrote home: "We shall have some fine fun next holidays reading plays over the fire-place". Lady Agnes wrote to Sir Henry when he was on his way to the West Indies:

29th December 1824

We spend all our evenings in the same way; dear William is the constant reader, Selina & Dick paste the newspapers & Grand Mama makes flannel waistcoats for her old Beaux...

Selina wrote: William has promised to bring Franklin's Voyage for us to read in the evenings...you must remember us too & fancy us round the Yule block or at our game of Commerce.

In January 1833 Judith told Sir Henry: "Mama is reading to us, Camilla, a novel, I believe, have you read it? It is rather pretty but not so amusing as your letters". Three years later, Anthony wrote, "I hear that the family Shakespeare has begun again. I remember the girls used to like it very much. Do they work at the same time?"

Children's Books

A small collection of books belonging to the Thornhill and Wager families suggests what was available to Derbyshire farmers' children in the 1860s and '70s. They are meant for children up to about eleven. They have many pictures; some are in rhyme and could be read aloud by an adult. Some were cheap, one or two pence. Others with hand-coloured pictures cost up to two shillings.

One of Routledge's Shilling Toy Books, The Peacock at Home, quotes a favourable review in The Standard of 23rd December 1870:

> No firm surpasses Messrs. Routledge in Sixpenny and Shilling Picture Story-Books. Could not be better drawn, printed or coloured if they cost twenty shillings instead of twelve pence.

One of the books in the collection was given to John William Thornhill, who wrote his name and the date in it – 27th September 1865. It was one of a series called *Frank Funny's Library*, and cost sixpence. The stories, in verse, were not perhaps as funny as the reader might hope, and could have been terrifying to some young readers. In one, Cruel Frederick

> ...killed the birds and broke the chairs
> And threw the kitten down the stairs...

but he ended up ill in bed.

The Dreadful Story About Harriet and the Matches tells how the pussy cats warned her not to touch the matches:

> Me-ow, they said, me-ow, me-o,
> You'll burn to death if you do so.

But she did, and, as illustrated with coloured pictures,

> So she was burnt, with all her clothes,
> And arms and hands, and eyes and nose,
> Till she had nothing more to lose
> Except her little scarlet shoes;
> And nothing else but these was found
> Among her ashes on the ground.

Another such horrible warning concerned little Suck-a-Thumb, who was told not to, but took no notice until a "great, long, red-legged scissor-man" came and cut off his thumbs "Snip! Snap! Snip!"

Some restraint was shown by Ward, Lock and Tyler in their *Child's Own Picture Colour Book:* the story of Little Red Riding Hood was told, omitting the Wolf. This normally cost one shilling, but was also available in an "Indestructible Edition on Strong Cloth" for two shillings. Nelson's Picture Books for Children were also advertised as "untearable". One wonders...

These picture books included traditional stories such as Mother Hubbard, and The Three Bears, but there were also some Scripture stories, such as David and Goliath, Joseph and the Coat of Many Colours, and Daniel. Reflecting the current belief in the value of Nature Study for children were *Walks with Mamma o'er Hills and Dales*, and *Eyes for Everything; or, How to Observe and What to Observe.*

Another pastime which the Wager family enjoyed on long winter evenings was a board game, *The Circle of English History.* The cards and the counters used in the game are missing, but the board with its important events in English History depicted in colour is still in good condition, with the instructions: The game proceeds until the Marriage of Queen Victoria [1840].

The cost of the books in the Wager collection, a shilling or sixpence, meant that they were beyond the reach of the poor, except perhaps one for a birthday or a Christmas treat. As well as the price being a deterrent, most of the poor, in Derbyshire as elsewhere, could not read, or could read only with great difficulty, and therefore did not read for pleasure. Illiterate or semi-literate parents could not read to their children, nor help them to learn, so it was not until a generation after the 1870 Education Act that a large juvenile reading public existed to give publishers the incentive to produce cheap books. Many of the first of these were "reward books" given for good attendance or achievement at day schools or Sunday Schools.

Plays and Charades

Children in families higher up the social scale sometimes made up a play or acted a charade for the adults to guess the word. The FitzHerbert children were not the only ones to enjoy play-acting. D'Ewes Coke's Diary for 1820 has the following unexpected entry:

4th January

The Children had Snap Dragon at night. William & Edward acted a play to us, of their own writing, which almost killed us with laughter.

In November 1866 Willie Turbutt suggested in a letter home: "Shall we get up a play next holidays? It would be rather fun". The most detailed account of a charade comes in a letter from Lady Agnes to Sir Henry in January 1833, when he was on his second visit to the West Indies.

At this time, Selina was married to Frank Wright, with a son, John, who was nearly two years old. The Wrights' Aunt Charlotte seems to have been "religious":

I wish you could have seen them the other night acting Charades. The word was Wheelwright and they broke down in a coach, the wheel rolling off, for the first syllable. Then Anthony and Judith entered, leading John on his knees, for Frank & Selina, and little John. Anthony quite a dandy, and Judith with downcast eyes for Mrs. Frank. Fanny was the Aunt Charlotte and set her little nephew upon a chair and began to question him: "Do you know, darling, about David and Solomon?" and "Do you think of them, dear?" It was so amusing; Fanny imitated Charlotte so admirably. This was to represent the Wright Family, and was all their own idea.

It goes without saying that none of the Wright Family were present at the performance.

Christmas

Christmas in the earlier part of the 19th century was a much quieter festival than it became later. This is reflected in Sir Henry FitzHerbert's Diaries. The first book which survives is for 1808, and from then up to 1834 there are no special remarks on 25th December. In 1834 the entry reads:

25th December

> Evening Service. Walked to Bentley Young Plantation with the children. Snap Dragon & Christmas gambols in the evening.

26th December

> Lady Fitz & I walked to...Mrs. Hardy's & Lady Fitz. then went to visit some sick persons in the Village.

The next specific reference comes in 1842, when he and Lady Agnes were staying with Selina and Frank Wright: "The Young Ones danced, had Snap Dragon, and much fun. Morning Service and the Sacrament".

In 1846 there is a single remark for 24th December: "Gussy made a Kissing Bush for The Hall".

Finally, in 1857, the entry in Sir Henry's Diary reads: "Christmas Day. We all went to Church. Alleyne preached a very good Sermon. All his Family dined with us".

One of the difficulties facing families wishing to get together for Christmas is mentioned in a letter which Selina wrote in 1836, explaining why she had not visited Tissington Hall with her family:

30th December

> ...we really would have brought them, if only to please the Grand Dad who I know loves to assemble all his children great & small around the Yule Block...I think you will see it is best to leave the little sprigs this time...another [coach] is snowed over out of sight...just while the Guard is gone for assistance, he comes back & no coach is to be seen.

Even with this disappointment, Christmas at Tissington Hall was a merrier occasion than at Brookhill, as these entries in D'Ewes Coke's 1817 Diary show:

Games, Hobbies and Holidays

Wednesday, 24th December

>   Sent the Boys a walk to Mansfield on Shop Errands. Walked with
>   Frances & Elizabeth to John Clarke's & John Stendale's cottages.
>   The Pinxton Singers came in the Evening.

Thursday, 25th

>   All walked to Church. I remained to receive the Sacrament.

Friday, 26th

>   Sent the 3 oldest Boys a walk to Alfreton. Elizabeth & I sauntered
>   about home, &c, for an hour.

Monday, 29th

>   Sent the 3 oldest Boys a walk to Mansfield.

Outings and Holidays

"Going on holiday" was an unknown concept in the early 19th century.
There were occasional outings, visits to relatives, and so on. When the
FitzHerbert boys were at Charterhouse Lord St. Helens sometimes
took them to a theatre, as he did in October 1824, when they saw
"Robroi" and "'Twould Puzzle a Conjuror". William reported that he
was "vastly amused".

In his Diaries, Sir Henry occasionally recorded taking some of his
children to plays or shows if they were staying in London.

12th August 1828

>   The 3 Boys & Maria & Judith went with me to see The Giantess, &
>   The Dwarf, & afterwards to the panorama of Rio Janeiro.

2nd October

>   ...went with Maria & John to the Lyceum to see The Bottle Imp &
>   The Blind Boy.

18th October

>   Lady Fitz., my Sister, Alleyne, Maria, Anthony, John, & Judith &
>   myself went to see The Tower.

18th July 1829

>   We went [with the boys] to see Tam O Shanter & the Panorama of
>   Sydney in New Holland.

Quite relaxing, then, to have more rural pleasures:

20th August 1830
    Spent the day with the Children in Dovedale.

There were many new industrial sites in the late 18th and early 19th century which children might be taken to see. D'Ewes Coke sent his boys "to descend the Coal Pits" in January 1820, and noted that they "were much amused with this subterranean expedition".

In February 1820 he and his sons, D'Ewes and Edward, went on another trip. He was actually taking D'Ewes to Shrewsbury School, but it was an opportunity to see "wonders". They went via Lichfield, Walsall and Shifnal. "It was quite dark when we reached Shiffnale but this prepared us very well for the Sight of Iron Bridge foundries &c., which were the most magnificent sight I ever beheld".

Later that year D'Ewes and William accompanied their father on a five-day tour, visiting Brimmington, Totley and Whittington, where he showed them "the Revolution House...and the old Chair there".

In 1839 Selina, then married, wrote to Lady Agnes inviting the family to join "an Expedition to Butterley" to see "the works & wonders of the place" and suggesting that "dear Gussy would be delighted to see the casting".

The great country houses which now attract thousands of visitors were also visited in the early 19th century, though they were not actually "open to the public" and there were certainly no children's playgrounds. In 1818 D'Ewes Coke showed his elder daughters, Frances and Elizabeth, around Chatsworth, on his way to meet D'Ewes at Bakewell. In July 1832 Sir Henry FitzHerbert and his family visited Chatsworth while they were on a three-day break. His record of expenses reveals a good deal about their adventures:

July 1832

		£ : s : d
19th	Housekeeper at Chatsworth	10 : 0
	Gardener at Ditto	10 : 0
	The Porter	2 : 6r
	Woman at Baslow Lodge	1 : 0
20th	Bill at Bakewell 3 days for 9 Persons	8 :14 : 6
	Waiter	10 : 0
	Bill for 4 Horses	1 :15 : 0
	Seeing Haddon	2 : 6
	A Mineral Specimen at Matlock	1 : 6
	Chimney Sweepers	3
21st	Specimens at Matlock	6 : 0
	Boatman	3 : 0

A large tip to the Housekeeper and Gardener took the place of an admission charge.

It is interesting to see that samples of rock were already on sale in Matlock, and the children must have enjoyed their trip on the river. Sweeps were supposed to bring good luck – but only if given a good tip.

The Seaside

The classic children's holiday now includes the sea, whether in Britain or further afield. This developed out of the practice of bathing in spa water, to cure diseases or simply to improve one's general health. Seaside towns which also had a spa were among the first to develop sea-bathing. Some people were enthusiastic enough to try drinking sea-water: not recommended.

> In October 1793 William Perrin wrote to his sister from Scarborough: "Your last letter came on Monday when I was at Robin Hood's Bay after drinking in the morning my usual quantity [of spa water]". As the weather was cold there were not so many people bathing, but "there are still however enough to employ 10 or 12 Machines before Breakfast & about as many between that & Dinner".

He also gave his opinion that "the mere shock of the Immersion of the Body into a Quantity of Water sufficient to cover it, is, if not too hot, a very salutary Thing..."

A visit to the seaside was still regarded as treatment rather than mere recreation in 1818, when Sir Henry and his family were staying at Beaumaris. An old friend wrote: "I shall be very glad to hear that...your Children have begun to derive the Benefit you anticipated from Sea Air & bathing".

In 1824 the FitzHerberts had a rather special holiday, perhaps because Alleyne had been very ill during his first term at Charterhouse and perhaps also because Sir Henry was due to sail to the West Indies in December.

The whole family went to Harrogate on 23rd July and stayed at the Granby. Next month they set out via Ripon, Helmsley and "Rixaux" Abbey, reaching Scarborough on the 25th. They stayed there about a week, went to Filey Bay on 1st September and then on to Whitby on the 10th. They travelled to York on the 12th, and then, as Sir Henry recorded in his Diary:

> On the 13th we took the whole Coach, The Express, to London, and started at 9 o'clock a.m. and we arrived in Town at 12 noon next day.

[One hopes a spare coach was put on for other would-be travellers].

Later in September Lady Agnes returned to Scarborough with the younger children, and reported to Sir Henry in London:

> Maria is looking very well indeed and has bathed twice. She eat an excellent dinner after & was in high spirits; all the rest well. Little Fanny has got the same rash on her arms, so she was not scorched...little Judith is to be a little Bathing Woman, the Sea agrees so well with her & she enjoys it so...we are rejoicing in this delicious sun for you in Town...it is also most favourable for the bathing.

The children's pleasure in the Seaside is well illustrated in a letter written by Anthony (9) in June 1827 to his mother who was in London while he and some other members of the family were staying at Farleigh:

> My dear Mamma,
>
> Nanny wants to know if we may go to Maidstone. You must say yes. Nanny and Grand Mamma and John to go in the Chariot and Me on Charles's Donkey if he'll lend it to me. Nanny says she can get horses for the Chariot at Mr. Phillpot's. You must say yes.
>
> yr affectionate
> A F

Games, Hobbies and Holidays

In July 1831 the FitzHerbert family stayed nearly the whole month in Ashby-de-la-Zouch "to try the Baths for Anthony". They had a fairly quiet time, riding and walking. On the 18th "walked last night after tea to Blackfordby". On the 22nd they drove to Staunton Harold and Calke Abbey. On the 28th "In the evening we went to hear Mr. Flemmington The Ventriloquist with Maria, Anthony, John, Judith & Fanny". One wonders if the children tried ventriloquism among themselves for the next few days.

The seaside holiday had become better established in 1852 when Frank Arkwright wrote to his grandmother, Lady Agnes, from Scarborough:

> 3rd August
>
> My dear Grandmama,
>
> ...I bathe every other day and have almost learned to swim. Harry says he is a coward, he will not bathe...Papa comes every week to see us and took me to see the wild animals, there were Lions, Tigers, Wolves, Leopards, a large Elephant and many other things that pleased me much to see.
>
> Your affectionate Grandson,
>
> Frank Arkwright.

A Visit to Buxton

Buxton was one of the earliest Spas in Britain, but not very suitable for children, at least not in 1891 when Adela and Isabel Strutt stayed there for a few days in February, at St Anne's Hotel.

Isabel began her letter home by saying: "It is very nice here", but she was merely being polite. She went on:

> ...we went to sea the golfing ground on friday. This morning we went to sea pools hole, a huge big cavern. We woudent go into it; it was rather dangerous. This afternoon we went to see "the cat and the fiddle" and Axehedge. I have seen a man with two noses. There are such a lot of nice things here. There is only a swimming bath for rheumatic people and no riding master...

Her next letter reported that "The pigeons in the pleasure garden are so tame they will sit on your cholder and eat out of your hand". On 2nd March her elder sister Adela joined her in Buxton and wrote her own account:

My dear Muddy,

We went out this morning, & this afternoon, & Isabel has smashed her umbrella & tell Nurse that she has smashed her scssors. We went to have some mineral water & went to the devonshire Hospittable to here the echo in the Dome.

A few days later Isabel wrote again.

We tasted the Curlibiate [Chalybeate] water. They said it was like milde Ink. It wasent...It is blowing here so I have no more to say.

With love from Isabel

A letter from Isabel

Brothers and Sisters and Parents

Dear Mother

Please thank Adela for the butterscotch & ask Isable if she would like some nougat or a box of cristilised fruits & tell her to share them with Adela.

George Strutt writing home from Prep School, 1889.

The FitzHerberts of Tissington

Brotherly and sisterly affection was often shown by giving presents. In his second year at Charterhouse William (13) wrote home: "Pray ask Selina if she wants any gloves for riding, because if she does Dick and I will give her a very knowing pair". In 1823 he asked, "Tell Selina we will bring back some of those flowers (I forget their name) when we come. Tell her to tell us the colours she should like". A little later William wrote to his father again:

> As next Saturday is Selina's birthday, I want you, if you are able to get me a pair either of dog skin gloves, or doe skin if she likes them best, the dog skins you can get in Burlington Arcade. Pray get me also some Hyacinths, some of the colours which Selina has not got. You may ask her what colours she has got (as it is no secret) and then get a few of the sorts which she has not got. The ones which we got before were 1s 6d apiece & so I think these had better be the same price. Pray get me also two for little Maria [7] whatever colours she likes best. Send our love to Mama & all the little children.

The wish to remember and give presents on birthdays lasted well beyond childhood. In October 1828 Richard was serving with the army in Canada, and wrote home:

> Today is Maria's birthday [12] pray tell her that I wish her many happy returns of it...I have got a little pair of Mocassins made for her by the Indian Chief's wife, they are very pretty, and have some little stars of Porcupine quills on the front. I have got a little canoe for the boys, nearly big enough to paddle in. I will bring them all when I come on leave.

Affection was also shown by remembering and sharing experiences. In 1829 Alleyne [14] wrote to his five year old sister Fanny: "I promised to write to you, and I am glad to hear that you like the lamp amongst the flowers in the drawing room because I liked it too". He added a note for Maria (12):

> I hope Judith [7]...helps to feed the hens and looks for the eggs and is a good helper to you and Johnny...and I suppose John looks at the Ferrets now and then and shows them to you and Judith...teach Judith the names of the hens.

In October 1825 William, then 17, wrote home from Charterhouse:

> I am very sorry that poor Maria [9] has got the tooth ache for I know by experience what a sad thing it is. I hope little Fanny [2] has now got over her maladies & that we shall have a happy & jolly christening at Xtmas.

Concern for brothers and sisters began at an early age. Maria (8) wrote to Papa in 1825:

> ...little Fanny has got three new double teeth and is very well, she tries to dance like Judith [3] and holds out her petticoats so drolly we wish you could see her, you would give her a good kiss.

This does not mean that the FitzHerbert children were always unnaturally polite to each other. Anyone was fair game for jokes and mock insults. Alleyne wrote to his father in June 1826, asking him to tell William and the others that "I am going to ride next Holidays like a fury, because Selina insulted me by telling me that Anthony and Maria would soon beat me".

In September 1826 Richard wrote to Selina:

> Alleyne is going to turn Shepherd. [He had asked William Johnson to buy him "a good sheep"]. We must buy him a pipe and a crook, tho' I think he is rich enough to buy it himself, as he very magnanimously says, he does not mind expense, but it must be good.

The fact that Alleyne wrote a note to Selina on the same sheet of paper shows that he was not very hurt by Richard's joke.

Alleyne was sometimes referred to as The Bishop, as he was intended for a career in the Church. Selina also had a nickname. In a letter to Maria in February 1828, Alleyne asked: "How is Slinky Selina?" The only other use of the name in writing is in a letter Selina wrote to her mother in October 1829, when they were both away from home. She ended a long letter with a frequent FitzHerbert sentiment: "Hourra for the day of our arrival at dear old Tissington!" And signed off with: "Ever Yr dutiful & affectionate Daughter, Slinky Fitz H-".

A letter from Anthony, at Harrow, in May 1834 shows how the good-humoured banter between brothers and sisters continued. "Tell the girls", he wrote to Sir Henry, "to send word all about Liverpool...when they have seen it, and [with heavy sarcasm] thank them all for their long letters, to me or John, I don't know which, as we can't read invisible ink".

The relationship between the children and their mother was clearly excellent, but there is little overt reference to it in the letters. Their father's place in their lives is much better revealed.

The tone of one of the earliest letters from William at Charterhouse to Sir Henry in December 1820 is something any parent will recognise. As William (12) and Richard (11) were due to come home on the Manchester Mail Coach, Sir Henry had announced his intention of meeting them at the School, and travelling with them. Panic! The embarrassment! How to persuade him not to?

> Dear Father,
>
> I am sorry to trouble you with another letter but I want to tell you about this going home. First of all I believe that the Manchester Mail is full of Charter House boys which I am sure you would not like...Nothing is more simple than what I am going to tell you. First of all, we must go by ourselves...we shall stay at the scool till a little before the time to set off, then we shall all get into a hackney coach with a Charter House servant who will pay our fare and see us all safe into the coach...we will promise not to eat eggs or muffins or any thing you would not let us eat. We would do the same as if you were there. Now then, I hope you let us go by ourselves as we will promise to be good lads. We will put on our flannel waistcoats and worthed [worsted] stockings and great coats. I will see that Dick puts his on and keeps his fingers out of mis-chief. I beg of you to let us go...[The other boys] would keep putting their Horns (those that went on the outside) and blowing, which you would not like but we should not care about...I hope that you will let us go. I know you are very good to us and always let us do anything that you think proper...

Several more lines of similar pleading and reassurances follow. There is no further reference to the matter but it is probable that the boys were allowed to travel unaccompanied.

Many letters survive which show how fond the children were of their father. In November 1824 Richard (15) wrote about Sir Henry's coming voyage to the West Indies: "I am afraid we shall be very dull without you...we shall in the mean take great care of our dearest mother, and I hope when you return we shall be the happiest set in England".

Even when Sir Henry was away from home for just a short time, the children wrote, urging him to return. In the summer of 1827, while the family were at Farleigh, Sir Henry was detained in London on business. Maria (10) wrote: "Do not stop any longer in London for we want you very, very sadly". Anthony (9) added: "I hope you are coming soon for I want you...we live very merrily but not half so merrily as when you are here". Three weeks later Maria wrote again:

> My dear Papa,
>
> I shall be very much obliged to you indeed & I will love you very dearly, if you will bring me a small knife with two blades, one broad, the other narrow. It shall not cut our love but add to it...I want very much to know what to say to make you come back to us. I think I must tell you what you said in one of your letters to me, that you would come to us & not leave us any more, & you must not teach your little children to tell stories.

She then signed off, adding: "Pray answer this by the return of the post & say if you will bring the knife". Even lady Agnes wrote (happily adding the note "en badinage") saying: "This is positively the last letter I intend to trouble you with". But the next day she confessed: "If I was to write no more...it would deprive me of my tip top pleasure during your absence".

Maria continued her rather "cheeky" relationship with her father.

In October 1829 Lady Agnes wrote to Sir Henry in response to a letter of his expressing concern that he was not at home to help them with their music studies:

> We have set down all the dancing & Music Lessons & are amused & affronted at your thinking we can do nothing without you. Maria says: What an old fellow he is! but when you come home we will forgive all.

At sixteen, congratulating Sir Henry on the birth of his second grandson, Maria ribbed him: "What an Old Grand Papa you are getting".

In June 1833, on hearing the news that Sir Henry was returning from the West Indies, Lady Agnes sent a letter, care of the Postmaster at Falmouth, saying "the good news...is better than any medicine, it is a sort of tumult of happiness throughout the House".

Very few of Sir Henry's own letters survive, but one, written "In the Downs off Deal, Friday afternoon 3 o'clock Novr. 26th 1824" is very important for the light it throws on his feelings towards the children.

It was sent to the boys at Charterhouse and begins with an account of the "hurricane of Tuesday last" with other ships wrecked, including "a large West Indiaman...on the Goodwin Sands" with some of the crew saved, including "a little Boy 10 years old".

He added other details of the ship he was on, and the crew, and how they had to sail back up the Channel from the Isle of Wight for safety. All exciting stuff which would appeal to William and Richard, and their schoolfellows. There was an account of their livestock.

> We have got on board a very nice Cow which has crossed the Atlantic once before...also some sheep, 7 or 8 pigs, plenty of Geese, Ducks and Poultry but I cannot say they are the most tender in the world.

Three of the geese escaped from their pen and flew away and "The poor Boy, a lad about 15, got a severe starting with a rope for his negligence". Other interesting matters: "Our Steward is a Black...One of our Passengers is a Barbadian Mulatto Gentleman, a sensible, well-informed man".

In a second letter written in May, from Jamaica, Sir Henry assured William:

> I completely entered into your feelings and alarms, when you began to read Thucydides, but I was sure that...the difficulties would vanish as you approached them. At the time of your examination...my heart was with you all three. [William, Richard and Alleyne].

He went on to explain how his estates had been accumulating debts through bad management. He had been able to correct this, and "My presence also has put an end to many evils affecting the Negroes, and we shall be able to introduce several regulations for the increase of their comforts".

The D'Ewes Coke Family

Relations between the D'Ewes Coke children were much less harmonious. One rare instance of brotherly love occurs in a letter to D'Ewes from William in July 1818. D'Ewes (14) was at school in Bakewell while William (12) was at home in Brookhill Hall:

> My dear D'Ewes
>
> I shall be very happy to take care of your garden...I mean to put some nice black earth in it...I will dig it and rake, and Frances will sow the seeds...I have Edward's garden to take care of too.

Sometimes their governess commented on a younger child's admiration for an older brother or sister – unfortunately for the wrong reasons. She noted on 3rd April 1818 how impressed Richard (5) was with William's running away from Risley Grammar School the previous November:

> I have frequently heard from the little girls how much Richard admired the conduct of his brother and of his determination to take the first opportunity of following his example...he has evidently imbibed the idea that insubordination and defiance of authority is highly becoming.

In August 1818 Sophy (10) was home from school with "a long list of school anecdotes" for Agnes (9) and Emma (7). On 30th August the governess noted: "...in her play she is boisterous...I have some reason to fear that when offended she is not scrupulous as to the language she uses". Her fears were confirmed on 2nd September: "When she thought I was out of hearing she began to talk to Agnes and Emma in a very improper manner. Her conversation was...a kind of impertinence indescribable, and only known to School boys and girls". One regrets Miss Burgess did not record Sophy's actual words.

The governess also noted some instances of fighting among her charges with Sophy usually the aggressor:

> Miss Sophia...has several times struck her sisters violent blows, and within this last two days in particular has given them, if not a black

eye, very nearly so...tho' I was present she contrived to make the injured party suppress their cries and coaxed them not to tell me...at one time she exclaimed "dear me, Emma, how you have been rubbing your eye". The next time, "Dear Agnes, how the flies torment you! How they get into your eye".

There were also complaints from the other children about Henry's (6) temper. Miss Burgess reported: "With me it shows itself in an obstinate stupidity; with them...in blows, or biting, pinching or scratching". On 23rd September 1818 she recorded a more serious incident:

> Master Henry has, in anger, thrown a large stone at Richard [5]. His sisters and Mary Goodall [a maid] saw him throw it...it slightly grazed Richard's cheek and a little bloodshed.

In his own Diary for 1820, their father commented on the elder boys' lack of friendship, regretting that "they do not like each other as they ought to do". They were also not on very good terms with their sisters, Frances and Elizabeth, two or three years older:

Wednesday, 5th July 1820
> The Boys either evaded, or refused to join their Sisters in their practising of Dancing lessons, for which I was obliged to speak very severely & to threaten then with chastisement if repeated.

As Harriet, D'Ewes Coke's wife, had died in 1815 there is little evidence on the quality of the children's relationship with her. A few letters to her from the elder girls when they were at school in Southwell mention pelisses and bonnets and a concert which they attended, but the tone is one of correctness rather than warmth of feeling. This could, however, be a result of their letters being "vetted".

D'Ewes Coke himself was very critical of the younger children, and we may suppose that they were respectful towards him, rather than warmly affectionate. His Diary for 1817 is full of unflattering comments:

January
> Emma [6] appears idle & trifling – awkward in the use of her knife & fork at table, forward in asking & greedy in eating.

> Edward [10] a very intelligent boy...as he does not show much courage at present...a classical education will suit him better than a military one.

Brothers and Sisters and Parents

D'Ewes [12] timid before his seniors & overbearing to his juniors, at present he appears little likely to make a manly soldier. He seems also constitutionally nervous & has some slight indications of asthma.

March

Agnes [7] will require infinite pains & vigilance to eradicate the seeds of artifice & evasion strongly rooted in her.

April

Agnes...inveterate idleness & duplicity.

July

Sophy [10]...perverse temper...

October

Emma [7] punished...for romping with John [the groom] & laughing when she joined Agnes after I had reproved her.

D'Ewes Coke's letters to his children are full of good advice and warnings, but little warmth. In August 1818, when D'Ewes was on holiday with relatives in Herefordshire, he had a letter from his father, hoping to have "an account of...how you pass your time" and going on with some advice:

> I hope you get up very early in the mornings. A boy should never be in bed at 6 o'clock – you should do some Exercises before breakfast, if nobody else is up, to keep them in your memory. There will be plenty of time in the day for play.

The exercises were not, of course, physical exercises, but "lessons".

In November 1818, D'Ewes (14) and William (13) were back at Dr Hodgson's, in Bakewell. Their father was as critical as ever: "You should not have sent back your Johnson's Dictionary for you do not spell well". "I think you have seen plays enough now, unless there should be one more...than Mr. Hodgson wishes you to see". But worse than bad spelling and a surfeit of plays was to come. A letter of 22nd November begins ominously "D'Ewes" instead of the usual "My Dear D'Ewes":

> I am very much surprized & grieved at a letter I have just received from Mr. Hodgson, in which he informs me that you have been to the Billiard table repeatedly, contrary to his known objection to it & to your promise not to go there. He informs me you have not

merely been there, but you have been playing, & have lost all your pocket money & have run into debt there besides.

I am most exceedingly hurt & angry at it – I could not have supposed a son of mine would have been so wanting in a proper sense of his honor & his duty to his tutor...It was mean & disgraceful to go there without his knowledge – It was worse still to go there to play, & worst of all to play without money to pay for the tables & to run into Debt to Strangers for it.

Some more follows along the same lines, and a note for William, instructing him to read the letter and apply the telling-off to himself. The letter is signed simply "D'Ewes Coke" – no "Affectionate Papa". Letters of abject apology from the boys have not survived, but the matter did not end there. A week later, their father sent another letter, directed more specifically at D'Ewes, and revealing even greater depths of wrongdoing:

My Dear D'Ewes,

I am very sorry to say you have been much worse than your Brother William in going to the Billiard table...He had the firmness not to spend more than 1s 6d there, & he would not play when he had no money...whereas you have been very often there, have run more into debt & have set your Brother the worst example you could...the whole of your conduct has been very discreditable to you, & it hurts me extremely to find you are so weakminded & have so little firmness or good principles...you have a debt also at Greaves's shop...tho' you have not been 2 months at Bakewell, in money & in debts you have spent 2 guineas already.

A few days later D'Ewes Coke went to Bakewell to see the boys, and must have been somewhat mollified by his sons' apologies. When he wrote again on 14th December it was to make arrangements for their return to Brookhill for Christmas. He was still critical of D'Ewes' spelling, however: "I desire you will look in your Dictionary how to spell Mayor, a Civil Officer, & Mare, a horse". And there was a warning:

I gave Mr. Hodgson a £1 note to pay your bill & William's at Greaves's & to give you the remainder...I will pay no more Debts that either you or William may be so shabby as to run into. You have both behaved very ill in that respect.

However, this letter is signed "I am your affectionate Papa, D'Ewes Coke".

Brothers and Sisters and Parents

Edward, apart from being labelled "does not show much courage" at the age of ten, seems to have escaped much criticism. When he did get into trouble, in March 1820, aged thirteen, he was quite unaware of what he had done wrong. His father recorded the incident in his Diary without the slightest hint that he might have handled it with a little more understanding:

> *Thursday, 30th March*
> Edward came home for Easter holidays. Poor fellow bought a Story which caught his eye in the shop window at Derby, called Emma, or the Consequences of Indiscretion, as a present to his Sister Emma [9]. I saw it in the School room and on reading it found two of the most scandalously indecent stories I ever read. I desired him to read what he had brought them & then burnt it – He cried much at his mistake.

The Longsdons of Longstone

It makes a pleasant change to consider the atmosphere in the Longsdon household. This was a farming family and the surviving letters are from an earlier period. The writers come across as being less at ease with pen and ink than the FitzHerberts or the D'Ewes Cokes. In spite of the slightly stilted style the warmth of family feeling is apparent in a letter sent by James Longsdon to his eldest son, at school in Heath:

> 12th Septemr 1799
>
> My dear James,
>
> This is the anniversary – but you will better understand me by saying your Birth Day. Your Mama has prepared Plumb-Pudding to which we are going to sit down – and shall then drink your health i.e. good wishes for your health and welfare and which will be extended to your brothers & I desire you will communicate to merry John & mild little William. The remembrance of you all three is not neglected to your Sisters. Prating little Kate calls out James & John & Gwillam. As soon as you all are capable of understanding how much it rejoices the hearts of your Father & Mother for you to be good and worthy Boys I am confident will merit our esteem. You are but Thirteen and the oldest. I pray God will prolong my life to train your Infant minds to the Love of Religion, Truth, Industry & Honour.

After some arrangements to see them, he concluded:

Present my most respectful Compts. to Mr. Ashbridge. Your Mama joins in love to you all

Your Affectionate Father

Ja: Longsdon

In November the boys' mother wrote to her youngest son:

My dear William

Your Letter gave me very great pleasure & your Papa thinks it very well written. I thank you for it...I sincerely hope...that we shall have the happiness of seeing you at Exms [Xmas] in good spirits...Your Cousin Mary Gardom is here. She unites with your Sisters in Love to you all...

I am my dear William very Sincerely Yours

E. Longsdon

Her husband added some remarks to all three boys, telling them to mind their books. For James he had some particular news:

I have to inform James that I have sold his Heifer with two others. She was valued at £12, it is less than I expected but the extream wetness of the Summer has been greatly against fatting Cattle...You must look about if you cannot find a nice barren Cow or two for the next Season, or a pair or two of good Bullocks that have had some Turnips.

A few years later James was at school in Nottingham. Now sixteen, he was taking a more adult interest in the farm and a more active part in the work when he was at home. His father wrote:

Longsdon 10th April 1803

I wish you was here for 3 or 4 days to see all the Cattle & assist us a little at this busy time...Tomorrow is Bakewell Fair...I will keep my letter open that I may inform you if I make any purchases. [The following day he added:] I have bought but two Cows & your Uncle John's Heifer. We have, I think, between 70 & 80 Lambs...[His mother added a note about his stockings, which had been made too small]. ...but if you cannot do without another pair...you must buy a pair...[and a message from his little sister] Katharine desires her best love, and her Ewe has lamb'd one pretty lamb today.

Brothers and Sisters and Parents

John William and Frances Dorothea Lace

John William Lace kept up a regular correspondence with his sister Fanny from 1841, when he went to a small private school, until 1849 when he was going up from Bromsgrove to Oxford. His letters have survived, hers not, but it is clear that they were very fond of each other.

John's letters are full of information, but they also show him as eager to amuse and entertain a sister two or three years older than he, who clearly made a satisfying response to news like the following in a letter of 14th September 1841:

> I have learnt a new game which I think you would like to know any number may play at it one person gives to the other each a peice of paper on which they are to write a question and on a very little bit of paper too, a noun. They then give their questions and the nouns to the same person who gave them the paper the person then changes the [word missing] from one paper to another and gives them back again. they are then to write an answer to the question and bring in the noun in the answer.

A letter in October 1841 begins

> My dear Fanny
>
> I am much obliged to you for your neice note.

After a few lines John announced: "I will now tell you a few riddles as I have nothing else". The quality of the riddles may be gauged from these examples:

Q. Why cannot you break an egg in an empty sack?

A. Because it could not be empty with an egg in it.

Q. What does a seventy-four gun ship weigh when it sets sail?

A. It weighs anchor.

John concluded: "If you like these riddles I will tell you some more in my next letter". Perhaps his sister politely refused, as no more riddles appear in later letters, but he was still signing off in 1842 "with loves & kisses to Mama, Elizabeth, Aunt & Cousins and yourself, I remain my dear Fanny, your affectionate brother, J.W.Lace". But, instead of riddles he was offering "to teach you a little Latin in the holidays".

The Turbutt Boys

William and Richard were separated by barely two years. As they were more or less at the same schools at the same time there are no letters between them, but judging by each one's references to the other in letters home, they were "best mates".

Most of their letters home were for Mama, and show a blithe relationship developing from the ages of 14 and 12 when they were at Harrow. Richard wrote on 13th February 1867, putting on a show of rage:

> You are very cool to take the young trout out of my aquarium and to comment on it in that manner that you did in your letter. [All this heavily underlined].
>
> I know what you will say when you read this, you will say You young humbug. It is all very well to say that. (What have you done with my mice?)
>
> I'll say that all the things in the hamper were awfully bad.
>
> With best love
>
> I remain
>
> Your affecte Son
>
> Richard

In his next letter he referred to unsigned Valentine cards which he and William had received: "I suppose you think we cannot read your writing. VALENTINES Thank you very much for them". In April William wrote to his mother: "In atonement for my former sin I write to you now a long letter".

Letters to Papa tended to be on more serious matters, and often included a reference to shortage of cash. Richard, in July 1871: "You are to come up to Lords if you please, it is at the end of this week...Will you please replenish my funds as they are getting very low".

Again, the following year:

> My dear Papa
>
> ...I wish you and Willie would come up and see me again before the end of the quarter [William had left Harrow]...Will you please send

me up a little money for my journey to Lords and back &c., as I have forgotten entirely to keep any for that emergency.

George Strutt, Adela and Isabel

One of the first letters that George wrote from Prep School in 1889:

May 22nd

Dear Adela

Thank you awffly for the sweates please thank Isable for hers and Muddy for her letter...

Spelling was not George's strong point, but sweets were, and the exchange of a wide range of sweets acted as tokens of love between George (10) and his sisters, Adela (12) and Isabel (8) while he was away at school. "Muddy" was, of course, mother, sometimes spelt Muddie. In tune with the period, Mama and Papa were out. George used "Mother" (if not "Muddie") and "Father" or "Daddy".

Sweets feature in many letters between 1889 and 1892:

Please thank Adela for the butterscotch & ask Isable if she would like some nougat or a box of cristilised fruits.

please thank Isable for the pencle & the goodies.

tell Isabel & Adela I am sending by next post a box of nougat and a box of chocolates between them.

Please thank Isabel and Adela for the chocolates and Lemon Kali. Please tell Isabel I am bringing them back a box of caramels, 1 box of nougat, a packet of armond rock and one of butterscotch.

Please thank Isable & Adela for the marangs & things.

Apart from exchanging sweets there are many other indications of good family relationships. George's letters to his mother were weekly, if not more frequent, and included queries about Daddy and thanks to him for books, money and other presents. George seems to have been consulted in other family matters too. On 21st May 1890 he wrote: "I think that Agnes Edith would be the nicest name for the baby".

At Christmas 1893, during an influenza epidemic he had to stay in bed in Harrow School, with his temperature around 100. His father visited him on 22nd December and George wrote to his mother: "It is very nice Daddy being here...It is so tiresome not being able to buy my Christmas presents for Adela, Isabel and the babies".

When his mother suggested that she should book into a hotel to be with him over Christmas he wrote back explaining (not very convincingly) that she would find it difficult to get anywhere to say, and adding:

> ...if you did come it would only spoil Adela's & Isabel's & the babies' Xmas, you see!
>
> Did Daddy get back home all right last night?
>
> With love to all, wishing a "very happy Xmas"
>
> Your loving son,
>
> George Strutt

Derbyshire Children at Home – Glossary

Affte – abbreviation for affectionate

Seals – decorative metal trinkets hung on a gentleman's watch-chain; could be used to imprint the wax when sealing letters

Signor Allegro – Mr Carefree

Bond – legal document guaranteeing a payment

Overseers of the Poor – Parish officials who gave money from the rates to people who could not support themselves.

Scantifyed – sanctified

Quadrille – square dance for four couples

Chaine des Dames – movement of a quadrille

Catechism – a set of questions and answers used in teaching the beliefs of the Church of England

Plump – plum

Bantom – bantam, a type of small hen

Phaeton Hood – the "boot" at the back of the carriage

A bag fox – a fox taken to the meet in a bag and then released, to guarantee a hunt

Lotto – a game of numbers, rather like Bingo

Loo – a card game

Commerce – card game with a "pool" of money to be won

Paste the newspapers – cut out interesting news items and stick them in a scrapbook

Charade – the "actors" choose a word of two or three syllables, e.g. "understand". They do a mime to suggest "under" and another to give a clue to "stand". They then act a piece which hints at the whole word. The "audience" must try to guess the word.

Snap-dragon – picking raisins from a bowl of burning brandy (you have to be quick!)

Glossary

Kissing Bush – decoration of evergreens and mistletoe

Panorama – wide view of a city or famous landscape painted on a roll of paper and unwound between two vertical cylinders.

New Holland – Australia

The Revolution House – where plans were made to invite William of Orange to take the throne from James II in 1688

Butterley casting – Butterley Ironworks

(Bathing) Machine – a small hut on wheels which was pushed into the sea. The female occupant could undress, enter the water, come out, and dress again with complete modesty

Bathing Woman – attended ladies in bathing machines

Chariot – light carriage

Thucydides – Greek Classical writer

Pelisse – lady's cloak usually with slits for the arms

Emma – novel by Jane Austen, 1815.

Money

£ - pound; gold coin, also called sovereign. (The capital L or £ came from the Latin word "libra" meaning a pound weight. A pound was worth 20 shillings or 240 pence.

s – shilling; silver coin worth 12 pence.

d – penny; copper coin. (The d was the initial letter of "denarius", a small coin in Roman times.

_ - halfpenny; small copper coin.

_ - farthing; very small, worth a quarter of a penny.

Gn – guinea; gold coin worth 21 shillings.

Note from the Publisher (a second-hand bookseller).

My rule of thumb for updating Victorian values or prices to their equivalent in the year 2002 is to multiply by 100. However while a shilling would have felt like much <u>less</u> than a "fiver" to the rich, it would have felt much <u>more</u> to the poor.

ALSO PUBLISHED BY SCARTHIN BOOKS

DERBYSHIRE CHURCHES AND CHAPELS OPEN TO VISITORS
Compiled by Rodney Tomkins, Illustrated by Elisabeth Stoppard, foreword by the Bishop of Derby
Illustrated paperback 128 pages ISBN 1 900446 02 2

TRANSFORMATION OF A VALLEY: THE DERBYSHIRE DERWENT
By Brian Cooper, photographs by Neville Cooper
Illustrated paperback 328 pages ISBN 0 907758 17 7

SQUIRE OF CALKE ABBEY: THE JOURNALS OF SIR GEORGE CREWE 1815- 1834
Edited by Colin Kitchling, foreword by Howard Colvin
Illustrated paperback 142 pages ISBN 0 907758 84 3

THE HISTORY OF THE DERBYSHIRE GENERAL INFIRMARY 1810- 1894
By V.M. Leveaux, foreword by Jeremy Taylor
Illustrated cloth-bound hardback 160 pages ISBN 1 900446 006

THE DIARIES OF MARIA GYTE OF SHELDON DERBYSHIRE 1913- 1920
Edited by Gerald Phizackerley, foreword by His Grace the Duke of Devonshire
Illustrated paperback 332 pages + 16 pages of plates
ISBN 0 907758 96 7

HANGED FOR A SHEEP: CRIME IN BYGONE DERBYSHIRE
By E.G. Power
Illustrated paperback 80 pp ISBN 0 907758 00 2

HISTORIC ORGANS IN DERBYSHIRE: A SURVEY FOR THE MILLENNIUM

By Rodney Tomkins, foreword by Nicholas Thistlewaite

Illustrated cloth-bound hardback 304 pages ISBN 0 907758 97 5

THE HOSPITALLER ORDER OF ST. JOHN OF JERUSALEM IN DERBYSHIRE HISTORY

By Gladwyn Turbutt

Illustrated cloth-bound hardback 64 pages ISBN 1 900446 01 4

ST. JOHN'S CHAPEL, BELPER: THE LIFE OF A CHURCH AND A COMMUNITY

By E.G. Power

Illustrated paperback 40 pp ISBN 0 907758 11 8

A STAGE OR TWO BEYOND CHRISTENDOM: A SOCIAL HISTORY OF THE CHURCH OF ENGLAND IN DERBYSHIRE

By Michael Austen

350 pp + 24pp Illustration (some colour)
paperback: ISBN 1 900446 03
cloth-bound hardback: ISBN 0 1 900446 04 9

DERBYSHIRE IN THE CIVIL WAR

By Brian Stone

Illustrated hardback 157pp, with notes, bibliography and index
ISBN 0 907758 58 4

http://www.scarthinbooks.demon.co.uk